PRAYERS
on My Shelf

(This Teacher's Praying!)

By Barb Quist

Chapbook Press

Schuler Books
2660 28th Street SE
Grand Rapids, MI 49512
(616) 942-7330
www.schulerbooks.com

ISBN 13: 9781943359714

Library of Congress Control Number: 2017947403

Copyright © 2017 Barb Quist
All rights reserved.

No part of this book may be reproduced in any form without express permission of the copyright holder.

Printed in the United States by Chapbook Press.

Table of Contents

Foreword xiii

Section One: Theme Prayers 1

Abide in Him 2

Administering Test 3

Administrator 4

Adversity 5

Agitated Parent 6

Assurance 7

Attendance 8

Attitude 9

Be Still 10

Bless Us 11

Break Time 12

Broken Families 13

Calm for Fears 14

Challenges and Opportunities 15

Clarity 16

Come Quickly 17

Compassion 18

Condemnation 19

Confession and Forgiveness 20

Confidence 21

Contentment 22

Control 23

Curriculum 24

Daily Grace 25

Daily Request 26

Delivering Special Lesson 27

Dependence 28

Dependence on Him 29

Desire Him	30
Discernment	31
Dissension in Staff	32
Distraught Student	33
District	34
Encouragement	35
Encouragement II	36
Encouragement III	37
Endurance	38
Evaluation Coming Up	39
Exhaustion	40
Faith	41
Feeling Helpless	42
Feeling Inadequate	43
First Day of School	44
God's Eyes	45

God's Presence	46
Good Health	47
Good Learning	48
Gratefulness	49
Help Me	50
Help Students	51
His Sufficiency	52
Hope	53
I Need Armor	54
Intersession	55
In the Morning	56
Joy	57
Lift a Burden Today	58
Lighten My Load	59
Listen to Him	60
Living Your Word	61

Look for Blessings	62
Love	63
Mercy	64
Mercy and Grace	65
Miracle Needed	66
Model for Colleagues or Student Teacher	67
My Families	68
My Family	69
My Heart	70
My Principal	71
Observation Today	72
Open My Hands	73
Open My Heart	74
Parent Blessing	75
Parents	76
Parent-Teacher Conferences	77

Patience 78

Patience II 79

Peace 80

Peace II 81

Peace in the Classroom 82

Phone Calls Home 83

Pleasing Him 84

Praise 85

Prayer of Jabez 86

Protection at Recess 87

Protection for Families 88

Protection for the Building 89

Protection from Outside Influences 90

Public Presentation 91

Renewal 92

Renew My Mind 93

Report Cards 94

Salt and Light .... .95

Seek Truth 96

Self-Control 97

Serve You 98

Stay with Me 99

Student's Last Day at School 100

Summer Vacation 101

Surrender 102

Surround Me .... .103

Tenderness 104

Thankful 105

Thanks for the Job 106

Thanksgiving 107

They Need You 108

Time 109

Tired	110
Trust	111
Vision	112
Who Can I Help?	113
Wisdom	114
Working for You	115
Worry	116
You Are Sovereign	117
Your Presence...	118
Section Two: Prayer of the Day	119
Monday	120
Tuesday	121
Wednesday	122
Thursday	123
Friday	124

Section Three: Read, Recite, Repeat 125

Read, Recite, Repeat Daily Scripture 126

Pick Your Mantra 128

Section Four: Devotions 129

It's All New 130

September Already? 131

Overwhelmed? 132

My New Heart 133

By Invitation 133

Sheep or Shepherd? 134

What's in A Name 136

Hangin' On 137

Keep Him Near 138

Easy Access 139

Seasons Change 140

Hold the Rod 142

Hand Written 143

A Bittersweet Goodbye 144

Thankfulness 145

Path of My Prayers .... .146

Time to Make Noise 147

Prayer 148

Ooo-Ooo Pick Me 149

Strength for the Asking 150

Free Courtesy Ticket 151

Meditate on This 152

Keys of the Kingdom 153

Focus 154

Kindness is a Secret 155

Who's in the Tree?. 156

Passion	158
Transformation	159
Changing a Stone	160
Not Meant to Be Like This	161
Be Still and Know That I Am God	162
From the Good Book	164
Ten Days Is Too Long	165
A New Coffee Pot	166
All in the Family	168
A Weekend of Praise with Michael W. Smith	169
Already There	170
Follow the (Your) Leader	171
Are You Happy or Joyful?	173
Fear	174
Finding Favor	176

His Plan for You	177
Parents at the Door	178
Stillness	180
References	182
Acknowledgements	183

Foreword

My first teaching job began after college graduation in 1971. It was a small farm community in Ohio. I had 35 first graders and no list of expected outcomes for the curriculum. The sixth-grade teacher was also the principal, and she asked me if I would teach art in addition to the first grade! As I had received a "D" in an art class in college (I was told the instructor could only give out a certain number of "A's"), I respectfully declined. I was sure 35 six-year-olds would be enough for this 22-year-old novice teacher. I was right.

The only thing I remember about that year was how much I didn't know, how little direction I felt, and the fact that I didn't feel God there with me nor did I think to invite Him in. Perhaps I would not have felt so helpless and weary if I would have sought strength from someone who could supply it. It was a public school after all, and what would God be doing there? Sure, I worshiped him in church, but I don't remember consciously taking him to work. And none of my colleagues talked about the Holy Spirit being present at East Elementary, in Upper Sandusky, Ohio.

Fast forward to 1994...by then I had been teaching in an urban setting for about eight years. I was challenged, busy, happy, and constantly uplifted by dedicated, hard-working teachers around me who were devoted to the idea of working with high needs, low income, disadvantaged kids. The teachers were smart, well educated, compassionate, eager, and totally in love with teaching; outstanding examples for me. But nobody talked about their faith or the need for strength, mercy, forgiveness, or prayer in our school. No God talk at all. Not until I met my young, faith-filled, student teacher.

We were working one hot August day preparing the room for the onslaught of first graders in a couple weeks and I was admiring her eagerness and excitement at the prospect of beginning her new career. I was indeed ready for a little shot of hope. She not only brought me hope, she opened a door for me which changed how I taught and how I got through the next seventeen years teaching in the city.

Bonnie began talking about God and faith and was witnessing to me. She was unassuming, casual, and acted as if she wasn't saying anything out of the ordinary. She might have had the same tone if she had been asking me where we were going for lunch or what I was doing after school. She was matter of fact and innocent and honest. She spoke to me from her heart. And she wore that on her sleeve. Bonnie was like a ray of hope for my room; as if she had just tossed me a life jacket in a storm.

I remember nodding and agreeing with her in our conversation as if I had been thinking the same thing when I was stunned and excited. From then on I had a comrade in the room. We had our faith in common and we were going to use it to summon help from the Perfect Teacher for one wonderful semester. And we did.

Of course, student teachers move on. We remained friends with limited contact as schedules were busy, but her gift remained with me. Some years after that as I became bolder in my witnessing at work. I asked some teachers if they wanted to pray together before school. There was no shortage of things to pray for: families in need, safety for students, good health…an endless list. I soon realized the teachers needed as much encouragement, uplifting, and protection as our kids. Our prayer time became one of reading a devotion and Scripture as well as praying. At 8:10 on Tuesday mornings, we would make an "all call" throughout the building and remind teachers and staff, whoever was available, to meet for a moment of quiet before our day began. This continued until I retired in 2011.

After retiring, I felt the Holy Spirit nudging. You know how that goes? He speaks and you say, "You want me to do what?" I visited my "old" principal over the summer and asked her if she would like me to return and pray with her before school each week. She could never attend our Tuesday morning devotions as she was always supervising the breakfast crowd or outside with students. I would pray with her on the fly sometimes but not with any regularity. Being retired, I could meet her in her office after she served breakfast and made her announcements. So, that was the plan...8:45 with the principal on Tuesday mornings. It seemed silly not to meet with the teachers too, since I could be there a little earlier and pray with them as well. Just like old times...8:10. The secretary was available at 7:45 so I went a little earlier to pray with her. The preschool teacher was available at 7:30 so I went still earlier to pray with her. It was a wonderful Tuesday morning.

That building wasn't the only one the Lord was calling me to visit. A few more nudges and four more schools were added. Sometimes my connection was a principal. Sometimes it was a secretary. Occasionally, three of us would meet, or it might be twelve. The Lord brought whoever needed his Word. I observed a host of faithful believers, thirsty for the Lord's blessing and His promise of strength at work, people eager to listen to words of encouragement and hope, words they didn't hear during their day in school. I remember feeling that way when I was teaching as well, but not until I was out of that environment, did I discern how acutely intense and overwhelming teaching can be.

Creating a book of prayers and devotions has been on my mind during these years of retirement. My intention was to write prayers with a direct purpose; meaningful and quick to grab (I know the frantic pace of teachers!). I also know the desperation that creeps in for hundreds of reasons all day long every day, every week. If we don't call on an all wise, loving, all powerful God to lift us up and guide and protect us, there isn't much hope for us to be effective, loving, teachers. I grew to rely on the Holy Spirit to direct my days as much as the schedule printed neatly on the board. I surrendered my teaching, my students, my families, my weariness, and any burdens I carried daily in my job, to the One who offered himself to me. Could I pray with my students? No, but I could pray FOR them. And I could pray for and with all the people in our building who would touch these students. If these kids were going to have a chance finding success at school, the Holy Spirit was the best Helper. It would be up to me to partner with Him and use his power in my weakness.

I pray that you find these prayers to be uplifting and encouraging. You are not alone in your classroom. You were never meant to be.

In His Light and Love,

Barb Quist

Section I

Theme Prayers

Abide in Him

Lord, today my prayer is that you will abide in me all day. Remind me continually that your arms are around me, sheltering me, holding me; protecting and guiding me. Let my hands be your hands and my words be yours. Direct my thoughts and let nothing evil take hold in this room today. I seek to feel your presence in and around me today.

Titus 2:11-14 (ESV)
For the grace of God has appeared, bringing salvation for all people, [12] training us to renounce ungodliness and worldly passions, and to live self-controlled, upright, and godly lives in the present age, [13] waiting for our blessed hope, the appearing of the glory of our great God and Savior Jesus Christ, [14] who gave himself for us to redeem us from all lawlessness and to purify for himself a people for his own possession who are zealous for good works.

Proverbs 16:9 (ESV)
The heart of man plans his way, but the LORD establishes his steps.

Psalm 73:26 (ESV)
My flesh and my heart may fail, but God is the strength of my heart and my portion forever.

Administering Tests

Anxiety is running high as students prepare to take tests this week (today.) I care about them and how well they do. I have encouraged them and have tried to motivate them to complete them carefully and thoughtfully. Many students will find the tests to be difficult and they will be discouraged. I pray you will calm their spirits and allow good thinking to occur.

Hebrews 4:15 (ESV)
For we do not have a high priest who is unable to sympathize with our weaknesses, but one who in every respect has been tempted as we are, yet without sin.

Hebrews 10:23 (ESV)
Let us hold fast the confession of our hope without wavering, for he who promised is faithful.

Psalm 33:4-5 (ESV)
For the word of the LORD is upright, and all his work is done in faithfulness. 5 He loves righteousness and justice; the earth is full of the steadfast love of the LORD.

Administrator

God of Mercy, I lift up (principal/administrator). I struggle in my relationship with him/her but respect him/her out of obedience and love for you. S/he's my boss and I'm accountable to him/her. I don't want to harbor ill feelings nor live with malice in my heart. Empty me of any hatred and replace it with a strong understanding of how I can work effectively with him/her. I surrender this burden to you.

Romans 8:16-17 (ESV)
The Spirit himself bears witness with our spirit that we are children of God, 17 and if children, then heirs—heirs of God and fellow heirs with Christ, provided we suffer with him in order that we may also be glorified with him.

Isaiah 41:10 (ESV)
Fear not, for I am with you; be not dismayed, for I am your God; I will strengthen you, I will help you, I will uphold you with my righteous right hand.

Psalm 37:23-24 (ESV)
The steps of a man are established by the LORD, when he delights in his way; 24 though he fall, he shall not be cast headlong, for the LORD upholds his hand.

Adversity

I sense adversity in my school environment. It comes through the families, the office, or sometimes through those around me. I pray you would protect us from this kind of evil today, that nothing would distract us from our mission for teaching and learning or our mission to serve you. Turn adversity into peace and let it thrive and spread from teachers to students to parents. Thank you for using your power for our good and your glory.

Hebrews 13:20-21 (ESV)
20 Now may the God of peace who brought again from the dead our Lord Jesus, the great shepherd of the sheep, by the blood of the eternal covenant, 21 equip you with everything good that you may do his will, working in us that which is pleasing in his sight, through Jesus Christ, to whom be glory forever and ever. Amen.

Ephesians 4:32 (ESV)
Be kind to one another, tenderhearted, forgiving one another, as God in Christ forgave you.

Psalm 100:5 (ESV)
For the LORD is good; his steadfast love endures forever, and his faithfulness to all generations.

Agitated Parent

I know how important it is to have a working relationship with the parents of my students. But today I am meeting with a parent that causes disruption and chaos in the office and sometimes attacks teachers verbally. Help me remain calm and sure; to listen but remain firm and strong. Let their ears be opened to truth and give me the words to allow progress to be made for the good of the student. Protect me from any attacks.

Romans 8:31 (ESV)
What then shall we say to these things? If God is for us, who can be against us?

Proverbs 18:10 (ESV)
The name of the LORD is a strong tower; the righteous man runs into it and is safe.

Psalm 27:1 (ESV) [1]
The LORD is my light and my salvation; whom shall I fear? The LORD is the stronghold of my life; of whom shall I be afraid?

Assurance

Thank you, Lord, for your assurance, your blessed assurance that Jesus is my Savior and my future in eternity is secure. Your Word tells us many times that we can know we are loved and you will never leave us or forsake us. Help me keep these words in my mind today as I battle all the challenges this day of teaching will bring. Keep your light of hope alive in my heart and let it shine for those around me.

2 Corinthians 5:17 (ESV)
Therefore, if anyone is in Christ, he is a new creation. The old has passed away; behold, the new has come.

Hebrews 13:15-16 (ESV)
Through him then let us continually offer up a sacrifice of praise to God, that is, the fruit of lips that acknowledge his name. 16 Do not neglect to do good and to share what you have, for such sacrifices are pleasing to God.

Psalm 139:1-2 (ESV)
O LORD, you have searched me and known me! 2 You know when I sit down and when I rise up; you discern my thoughts from afar.

Attendance

Attendance is poor in our building. It's hard enough to teach where the needs are extreme but it's impossible when the attendance is not a priority. Help our families see that attendance at school is the first best thing they can do to help their children succeed. Help them take this responsibility seriously so their kids get the chance they need at school.

2 Thessalonians 3:5 (ESV)
May the Lord direct your hearts to the love of God and to the steadfastness of Christ.

2 Chronicles 7:14 (ESV)
if my people who are called by my name humble themselves, and pray and seek my face and turn from their wicked ways, then I will hear from heaven and will forgive their sin and heal their land.

Psalm 84:11 (ESV)
For the LORD God is a sun and shield; the LORD bestows favor and honor. No good thing does he withhold from those who walk uprightly.

Attitude

Make my attitude like that of Jesus. Help me see truth and be a good listener. Make me slow to anger and keep a guard over my lips. I want to be a good servant and represent Christ on this earth but my human nature is powerful and often wins. Keep your Spirit alive and strong, squelching anything that is not from you.

Romans 3:21-24 (ESV)
But now the righteousness of God has been manifested apart from the law, although the Law and the Prophets bear witness to it— 22 the righteousness of God through faith in Jesus Christ for all who believe. For there is no distinction: 23 for all have sinned and fall short of the glory of God, 24 and are justified by his grace as a gift, through the redemption that is in Christ Jesus,

Habakkuk 3:17-19 (ESV)
Though the fig tree should not blossom, nor fruit be on the vines, the produce of the olive fail and the fields yield no food, the flock be cut off from the fold and there be no herd in the stalls, 18 yet I will rejoice in the LORD; I will take joy in the God of my salvation. 19 GOD, the Lord, is my strength; he makes my feet like the deer's; he makes me tread on my high places. To the choirmaster: with stringed instruments.

Psalm 121:1-2 (ESV)
I lift up my eyes to the hills. From where does my help come? 2 My help comes from the LORD, who made heaven and earth.

Be Still

It's hard, Lord, to find the time in the day to be still and quiet enough to hear what you are saying. Help me find that time when I close out the world around me and focus my eyes and my heart on you. I don't want to miss your words to me as it's only you that guides me.

Colossians 4:2 (ESV)
Continue steadfastly in prayer, being watchful in it with thanksgiving.

Ephesians 6:14-15 (ESV)
Stand therefore, having fastened on the belt of truth, and having put on the breastplate of righteousness, [15] and, as shoes for your feet, having put on the readiness given by the gospel of peace.

Psalm 46:10 (ESV)
"Be still, and know that I am God. I will be exalted among the nations, I will be exalted in the earth!"

Bless Us

Bless this room, Gracious God. Let your Spirit touch all the hearts that walk through my door. Let peace and good learning prevail and let us feel your presence in every hour.

Romans 12:18 (ESV)
If possible, so far as it depends on you, live peaceably with all.

Acts 2:28 (ESV)
You have made known to me the paths of life; you will make me full of gladness with your presence.'

Psalm 143:8 (ESV)
Let me hear in the morning of your steadfast love, for in you I trust. Make me know the way I should go, for to you I lift up my soul.

Break Time

God of Peace, I take this time to settle my mind and reflect. The kids are demanding and there doesn't seem to be a moment during my day where they aren't asking me for something. So I sit alone with you and pray for quiet; a stillness where I can hear only you. Thank you for this break. Allow it to refresh me so I can return to my students with renewed energy.

Colossians 3:15 (ESV)
And let the peace of Christ rule in your hearts, to which indeed you were called in one body. And be thankful.

Deuteronomy 30:20 (ESV)
… loving the LORD your God, obeying his voice and holding fast to him, for he is your life and length of days

Psalm 145:3-5 (ESV)
Great is the LORD, and greatly to be praised, and his greatness is unsearchable. [4] One generation shall commend your works to another, and shall declare your mighty acts. [5] On the glorious splendor of your majesty, and on your wondrous works, I will meditate.

Broken Families

I meet moms and dads every day who struggle through each day with heavy burdens. Some of them know you and some are still wandering. I am asking you to speak to the parents who know you and invite them to lay their burdens at your cross. Meet the ones who don't know you or your mercies and draw them to you that they may know your comfort, forgiveness and the joy you offer. Heal these parents, Lord, in Jesus' name.

Philippians 2:3-4 (ESV)
Do nothing from selfish ambition or conceit, but in humility count others more significant than yourselves. 4 Let each of you look not only to his own interests, but also to the interests of others.

2 Peter 1:5-7 (ESV)
For this very reason, make every effort to supplement your faith with virtue, and virtue with knowledge, and knowledge with self-control, and self-control with steadfastness, and steadfastness with godliness, and godliness with brotherly affection, and brotherly affection with love.

Psalm 32:8 (ESV)
I will instruct you and teach you in the way you should go; I will counsel you with my eye upon you.

Calm for Fears

Sometimes this job overwhelms me and fear creeps in. I let circumstances and even other people take your place and I am afraid. My work is affected by misplaced fear and I know only redirecting my focus to you will adjust my heart and dispel all fear. Remove all fear and replace it with a deeper trust in you, Holy God. I know you have promised to be with me.

Proverbs 29:25 (ESV)
The fear of man lays a snare, but whoever trusts in the LORD is safe.

Hebrews 3:1-2 (ESV)
Therefore, holy brothers, you who share in a heavenly calling, consider Jesus, the apostle and high priest of our confession, 2 who was faithful to him who appointed him, just as Moses also was faithful in all God's house.

Psalm 29:11 (ESV)
May the LORD give strength to his people! May the LORD bless his people with peace!

Challenges and Opportunities

I pray as challenges and opportunities come my way today, you will give me what I need to meet them. I'll need your strength and wisdom and I call upon the power you've placed in me through the Spirit that lives in me to guide my words, decisions, and the outcomes. Bless my efforts today that you may be glorified through me.

Philippians 4:4-7 (ESV)
Rejoice in the Lord always; again I will say, rejoice. 5 Let your reasonableness be known to everyone. The Lord is at hand; 6 do not be anxious about anything, but in everything by prayer and supplication with thanksgiving let your requests be made known to God. 7 And the peace of God, which surpasses all understanding, will guard your hearts and your minds in Christ Jesus.

Colossians 3:17 (ESV)
And whatever you do, in word or deed, do everything in the name of the Lord Jesus, giving thanks to God the Father through him.

Psalm 52:9 (ESV)
I will thank you forever, because you have done it. I will wait for your name, for it is good, in the presence of the godly.

Clarity

Lord, sometimes the speed of my days and the myriad of obligations blur my vision and my days have no clarity. My path becomes cluttered and true meaning is clouded. Give me clarity today, Lord, and remove what's blinding me from your vision for me. Give me the power of discernment so I can see clearly the order in my day. I give you thanks for this blessing.

John 10:27-28 (ESV)
My sheep hear my voice, and I know them, and they follow me. [28] I give them eternal life, and they will never perish, and no one will snatch them out of my hand.

Romans 15:13 (ESV)
May the God of hope fill you with all joy and peace in believing, so that by the power of the Holy Spirit you may abound in hope.

Psalm 37:5 (ESV)
Commit your way to the LORD; trust in him, and he will act.

Come Quickly

Heavenly Father, this is an emergency. I am aware of an abuse; an injustice towards one of your children and I can't handle it alone. You could intervene and let justice reign. I commend this situation to you.

Romans 8:15-17 (ESV)
For you did not receive the spirit of slavery to fall back into fear, but you have received the Spirit of adoption as sons, by whom we cry, "Abba! Father!" 16 The Spirit himself bears witness with our spirit that we are children of God, 17 and if children, then heirs— heirs of God and fellow heirs with Christ, provided we suffer with him in order that we may also be glorified with him.

Job 28:12 (ESV)
"But where shall wisdom be found? And where is the place of understanding?

Psalm 51:6 (ESV)
Behold, you delight in truth in the inward being, and you teach me wisdom in the secret heart.

Compassion

Merciful Father, You sent your Son as a model of compassion. I'm asking for that same compassion today as I deal with students and all others in my path. Help me see them through your eyes and where I am weak, perfect me with the compassion of Christ.

Matthew 22:37-39 (ESV)
And he said to him, "You shall love the Lord your God with all your heart and with all your soul and with all your mind. 38 This is the great and first commandment. 39 And a second is like it: You shall love your neighbor as yourself.

John 3:16-17 (ESV)
For God so loved the world, that he gave his only Son, that whoever believes in him should not perish but have eternal life. 17 For God did not send his Son into the world to condemn the world, but in order that the world might be saved through him.

Psalm 90:14 (ESV)
Satisfy us in the morning with your steadfast love, that we may rejoice and be glad all our days.

Condemnation

I know under your blanket of righteousness I stand in your love; there is no condemnation. Release me and keep me focused on the One who knows truth and is truth. Protect me from the enemies' arrows.

1 John 5:14 (NRSV)
And this is the boldness we have in him, that if we ask anything according to his will, he hears us.

Matthew 19:26 (ESV)
But Jesus looked at them and said, "With man this is impossible, but with God all things are possible."

Psalm 119:35 (ESV)
Lead me in the path of your commandments, for I delight in it.

Confession and Forgiveness

I trust in your faithfulness and promise of forgiveness. I mess up every day and need a second chance. Forgive the words I used to tear someone down and help them be restored and built up. Forgive any actions that didn't show love or understanding and heal the harm I have done. Forgive impure thoughts I have and replace them with what is right and noble. Make me an example of your love and help me forgive others so you forgive me.

John 14:1 (ESV)
"Let not your hearts be troubled. Believe in God; believe also in me.

Ephesians 3:14-19 (ESV)
14 For this reason I bow my knees before the Father, 15 from whom every family in heaven and on earth is named, 16 that according to the riches of his glory he may grant you to be strengthened with power through his Spirit in your inner being, 17 so that Christ may dwell in your hearts through faith—that you, being rooted and grounded in love, 18 may have strength to comprehend with all the saints what is the breadth and length and height and depth, 19 and to know the love of Christ that surpasses knowledge, that you may be filled with all the fullness of God.

Psalm 119:10-12 (ESV)
With my whole heart I seek you; let me not wander from your commandments! 11 I have stored up your word in my heart, that I might not sin against you. 12 Blessed are you, O LORD; teach me your statutes!

Confidence

I stand in front of my classroom every day and try to be the kind of leader that would honor you. But sometimes the responsibility is overwhelming and I falter in my confidence under the pressure. Ignite a confidence in me where your face will shine and someone will see you today in my teaching. I surrender my lessons to you, God, and depend on your arms to uphold me.

1 Peter 2:24-25 (NRSV)
He himself bore our sins in his body on the cross, so that, free from sins, we might live for righteousness; by his wounds you have been healed. [25] For you were going astray like sheep, but now you have returned to the shepherd and guardian of your souls.

2 Corinthians 9:8 (ESV)
And God is able to make all grace abound to you, so that having all sufficiency in all things at all times, you may abound in every good work.

Psalm 46:1-3 (ESV)
God is our refuge and strength, a very present help in trouble. [2] Therefore we will not fear though the earth gives way, though the mountains be moved into the heart of the sea,
[3] though its waters roar and foam, though the mountains tremble at its swelling. Selah

Contentment

I know we are to be content wherever we are and in all circumstances. Help me keep my eyes on what's important today; things I can control, things assigned to me. Let me be content with my responsibilities while being supportive of others. Help me not to shirk or avoid but persevere towards my goals for the day. Grant me your blessing today.

Jeremiah 33:3 (ESV)
Call to me and I will answer you, and will tell you great and hidden things that you have not known.

1 Corinthians 2:9-10 (ESV)
But, as it is written, "What no eye has seen, nor ear heard, nor the heart of man imagined, what God has prepared for those who love him"— 10 these things God has revealed to us through the Spirit. For the Spirit searches everything, even the depths of God.

Psalm 18:30 (ESV)
This God—his way is perfect; the word of the LORD proves true; he is a shield for all those who take refuge in him.

Control

I struggle all day to gain control. It is necessary in our classroom if good learning and good teaching are going on. But I know in my heart that only you are in control. Give me your perfect wisdom and strength to surrender my control to you; that you would be the One in charge of students and teachers alike. Direct our path today so that everything we do is for our good and your glory.

1 John 5:14-15 (NRSV)
And this is the boldness we have in him, that if we ask anything according to his will, he hears us. 15 And if we know that he hears us in whatever we ask, we know that we have obtained the requests made of him.

Micah 6:8 (ESV)
He has told you, O man, what is good; and what does the LORD require of you but to do justice, and to love kindness, and to walk humbly with your God?

Psalm 119:35 (ESV)
Lead me in the path of your commandments, for I delight in it.

Curriculum

I am thankful to be teaching in a place where we have many books and supplies available. We have a comfortable classroom and teaching is often a pleasure. But Lord, my students come to me far behind where the district says they should be academically. They are often ill prepared for the level of instruction in our room at this grade and because it is difficult, they get discouraged and often end up off task. Poor behavior becomes the rule rather than the exception. Lord, help me find ways to close the gap in their learning and give them teachable spirits. Extend this to all the rooms in our building, Lord, and may you be glorified.

1 Peter 2:21 (ESV)
For to this you have been called, because Christ also suffered for you, leaving you an example, so that you might follow in his steps.

Luke 1:37 (ESV)
For nothing will be impossible with God."

Psalm 5:6-8 (ESV)
You destroy those who speak lies; the LORD abhors the bloodthirsty and deceitful man. 7 But I, through the abundance of your steadfast love, will enter your house. I will bow down toward your holy temple in the fear of you. 8 Lead me, O LORD, in your righteousness because of my enemies; make your way straight before me.

Daily Grace

I thank you, Lord, for a night of rest and a day of new beginnings. I look forward to the opportunities and challenges I will find today and pray that you have equipped me to meet them all. Give me your heart today as I greet my students so your love fills each one of them. Give me your perfect wisdom as I teach and let everyone in my care feel your peace. I won't be strong enough to shoulder everything that will come my way so I will be depending totally on your strength today.

1 Peter 1:3-5 (ESV)
Blessed be the God and Father of our Lord Jesus Christ! According to his great mercy, he has caused us to be born again to a living hope through the resurrection of Jesus Christ from the dead, 4 to an inheritance that is imperishable, undefiled, and unfading, kept in heaven for you, 5 who by God's power are being guarded through faith for a salvation ready to be revealed in the last time.

2 Thessalonians 3:5 (ESV)
May the Lord direct your hearts to the love of God and to the steadfastness of Christ.

Psalm 42:8 (ESV)
By day the LORD commands his steadfast love, and at night his song is with me, a prayer to the God of my life.

Daily Request

Open my ears and fill my mind and my heart with only you today, Lord.

Ephesians 3:20-21 (ESV)
Now to him who is able to do far more abundantly than all that we ask or think, according to the power at work within us, 21 to him be glory in the church and in Christ Jesus throughout all generations, forever and ever. Amen.

2 Corinthians 10:3-5 (ESV)
For though we walk in the flesh, we are not waging war according to the flesh. 4 For the weapons of our warfare are not of the flesh but have divine power to destroy strongholds. 5 We destroy arguments and every lofty opinion raised against the knowledge of God, and take every thought captive to obey Christ,

Psalm 37:7 (ESV)
Be still before the LORD and wait patiently for him; fret not yourself over the one who prospers in his way, over the man who carries out evil devices!

Delivering Special Lesson

I am delivering a special lesson today and am asking for your added blessing on my words and actions. It is not my desire that I be the focus but that clear understanding and good learning are the outcomes. Open the hearts and minds of those watching and hearing this lesson. I pray that it is for my good and your glory.

Matthew 6:33-34 (ESV)
But seek first the kingdom of God and his righteousness, and all these things will be added to you. 34 "Therefore do not be anxious about tomorrow, for tomorrow will be anxious for itself. Sufficient for the day is its own trouble.

2 Peter 1:3 (ESV)
His divine power has granted to us all things that pertain to life and godliness, through the knowledge of him who called us to his own glory and excellence,

Psalm 149:4 (ESV)
For the LORD takes pleasure in his people; he adorns the humble with salvation.

Dependence

I declare my complete dependence on you, Lord. I know you will meet me in my weakness to perfect my work today. You will be my strength, my encouragement and the source of my joy. I surrender each hour to you. Direct my time and energy today so everything I do will be for my good and your glory.

Exodus 33:14 (ESV)
And he said, "My presence will go with you, and I will give you rest."

Jude 1:24-25 (ESV)
Now to him who is able to keep you from stumbling and to present you blameless before the presence of his glory with great joy, 25 to the only God, our Savior, through Jesus Christ our Lord, be glory, majesty, dominion, and authority, before all time and now and forever. Amen.

Psalm 28:7 (ESV)
The LORD is my strength and my shield; in him my heart trusts, and I am helped; my heart exults, and with my song I give thanks to him.

Dependence on Him

I rush through my day at school trying to keep things in order and under control. When there are no crises and things are quiet and smooth, I get a sense of self-reliance and my head tells me I'm doing a good job. But when things begin to crumble and I'm scrambling to regain decorum, I immediately turn my eyes to you and begin begging. Show me Lord, that it is always you in control; that I am always totally dependent on you. I don't want to rely on my own strength, but yours.

Romans 9:16 (ESV)
So then it depends not on human will or exertion, but on God, who has mercy.

Romans 8:37-39 (ESV)
No, in all these things we are more than conquerors through him who loved us. 38 For I am sure that neither death nor life, nor angels nor rulers, nor things present nor things to come, nor powers, 39 nor height nor depth, nor anything else in all creation, will be able to separate us from the love of God in Christ Jesus our Lord.

Psalm 62:9 (ESV)
Those of low estate are but a breath; those of high estate are a delusion; in the balances they go up; they are together lighter than a breath.

Desire Him

Sometimes I'm too busy during the day to even know what I want, much less what I need. Increase my desire for you. Help me include you in everything I do and every word I say throughout the day. I pray that even while I'm teaching, my words may somehow reflect my love for you bringing someone closer to you.

Romans 8:28 (ESV)
And we know that for those who love God all things work together for good, for those who are called according to his purpose.

Romans 7:18 (ESV)
For I know that nothing good dwells in me, that is, in my flesh. For I have the desire to do what is right, but not the ability to carry it out.

Psalm 73:25 (ESV)
Whom have I in heaven but you? And there is nothing on earth that I desire besides you.

Discernment

I am bombarded with questions and find myself in situations all day where I need good judgment. Grow in me the ability to discern right from wrong; your will from mine. Bring calm and peace where there is none and let me be an instrument of that peace.

Matthew 5:16 (ESV)
In the same way, let your light shine before others, so that they may see your good works and give glory to your Father who is in heaven.

Romans 5:1-2 (ESV)
Therefore, since we have been justified by faith, we have peace with God through our Lord Jesus Christ. 2 Through him we have also obtained access by faith into this grace in which we stand, and we rejoice in hope of the glory of God.

Psalm 86:4 (ESV)
Gladden the soul of your servant, for to you, O Lord, do I lift up my soul.

Dissension in Staff

O God of All Peace, You alone have the power to calm storms and return the waters to stillness. Look at our staff. Heal us and restore a working relationship. Open hearts and minds and allow your balm of tranquility to wash over us. We seek to glorify you in all we do.

Colossians 3:12-13 (ESV)
Put on then, as God's chosen ones, holy and beloved, compassionate hearts, kindness, humility, meekness, and patience, [13] bearing with one another and, if one has a complaint against another, forgiving each other; as the Lord has forgiven you, so you also must forgive.

1 Peter 4:10-11 (ESV)
[1] As each has received a gift, use it to serve one another, as good stewards of God's varied grace:
[11] whoever speaks, as one who speaks oracles of God; whoever serves, as one who serves by the strength that God supplies—in order that in everything God may be glorified through Jesus Christ. To him belong glory and dominion forever and ever. Amen.

Psalm 31:19-20 (ESV)
Oh, how abundant is your goodness, which you have stored up for those who fear you and worked for those who take refuge in you, in the sight of the children of mankind!
[20] In the cover of your presence you hide them from the plots of men; you store them in your shelter from the strife of tongues.

Distraught Student

Merciful Father, I lift (name of student) to you. You know what's going on with (his/her) life and I know you are in control. There seem to be so many issues that prohibit learning and stand in the way of progress. Look down on (name) with your mercy. Guide the family to support (him/her) positively and let our classroom be a haven of healing for (him/her.) Grant me insight and discernment to be what (s/he) needs at school. Thank you for bringing (him/her) to me.

Jeremiah 33:3 (ESV)
Call to me and I will answer you, and will tell you great and hidden things that you have not known.

Joshua 1:9 (ESV)
Have I not commanded you? Be strong and courageous. Do not be frightened, and do not be dismayed, for the LORD your God is with you wherever you go.

Psalm 31:24 (ESV)
Be strong, and let your heart take courage, all you who wait for the LORD!

District

I lift up everyone who works honestly and diligently for our district. There is so much I don't see from my classroom and the problems they deal with in administrative offices are different from mine. Let your Spirit move about in conversations and meetings, directing decisions and policies. Open eyes to fairness and what is right for all our students. Bless our superintendent and give her/him unending wisdom to know what's best for our school system and our kids. Grant our schools your mercy.

Proverbs 9:10 (ESV)
The fear of the LORD is the beginning of wisdom, and the knowledge of the Holy One is insight.

Isaiah 12:2 (ESV)
Behold, God is my salvation; I will trust, and will not be afraid; for the LORD GOD is my strength and my song, and he has become my salvation.

Psalm 18:1-2 (ESV)
I love you, O LORD, my strength. 2 The LORD is my rock and my fortress and my deliverer, my God, my rock, in whom I take refuge, my shield, and the horn of my salvation, my stronghold.

Encouragement

Lord, I watch the faces of my students as I teach. I try to deliver my lessons with words of truth, compassion, and sound instruction. But what I see is confusion and frustration and poor behavior creeps in. The meaning is lost as I deal with those who are robbing others of good learning. Lord, fill each student with a yearning, a curiosity; the motivation and encouragement they all need to be successful learners. Keep their hearts and minds open to what is important at school.

Mark 11:24 (ESV)
Therefore I tell you, whatever you ask in prayer, believe that you have received it, and it will be yours.

Jeremiah 31:25 (ESV)
For I will satisfy the weary soul, and every languishing soul I will replenish."

Psalm 18:28 (ESV)
For it is you who light my lamp; the LORD my God lightens my darkness.

Encouragement II

Sometimes I deliver a lesson and my students seem to ignore me or are disruptive. They show no evidence of caring or interest. Take away my pride and empower me with the ability to reach and teach all those in my class today.

2 Samuel 22:34 (ESV)
He made my feet like the feet of a deer and set me secure on the heights.

Zephaniah 3:17 (ESV)
The LORD your God is in your midst, a mighty one who will save; he will rejoice over you with gladness; he will quiet you by his love; he will exult over you with loud singing.

Psalm 131:2 (ESV)
But I have calmed and quieted my soul, like a weaned child with its mother; like a weaned child is my soul within me.

Encouragement III

Keep my eyes on you today, Lord, that I might draw my strength and encouragement from you. Sustain me so I can be the same encouragement to my students and fellow teachers. Help me point to you in all my words and actions. It's you I trust and seek. Your promises are true and you won't leave me. Thank you for this assurance.

John 14:15-17 (ESV)
If you love me, you will keep my commandments. 16 And I will ask the Father, and he will give you another Helper, to be with you forever, 17 even the Spirit of truth, whom the world cannot receive, because it neither sees him nor knows him. You know him, for he dwells with you and will be in you.

Exodus 15:2 (ESV)
The LORD is my strength and my song, and he has become my salvation; this is my God, and I will praise him, my father's God, and I will exalt him.

Psalm 62:1-2 (ESV)
For God alone my soul waits in silence; from him comes my salvation. 2 He alone is my rock and my salvation, my fortress; I shall not be greatly shaken.

Endurance

The race is long today. I'm weary and each hour brings me closer to my knees. I want to surrender and give up the course I'm on. Remind me of your promise to lift me; stay with me and sustain me. Use me today, Lord, to point someone to Jesus and strengthen me that I might again feel the joy that only comes from you.

Exodus 15:2 (ESV)
The LORD is my strength and my song, and he has become my salvation; this is my God, and I will praise him, my father's God, and I will exalt him.

Psalm 46:1 (ESV)
God is our refuge and strength, a very present help in trouble.

Psalm 105:4 (ESV)
Seek the LORD and his strength; seek his presence continually!

Evaluation Coming Up

You know my heart and how hard I work and how I love my job. I seek to honor you and follow your will. Give me the encouragement and trust I need as others judge me. Let me exhibit your calm and assurance that I am doing the best I can do. Take away all anxiety and replace it with inner peace. Make my room a haven for learning and bless all who observe me today. It's you I want to please, Lord.

Colossians 1:28-29 (ESV)
Him we proclaim, warning everyone and teaching everyone with all wisdom, that we may present everyone mature in Christ. 29 For this I toil, struggling with all his energy that he powerfully works within me.

1 Peter 5:6-7 (ESV)
Humble yourselves, therefore, under the mighty hand of God so that at the proper time he may exalt you, 7 casting all your anxieties on him, because he cares for you.

Psalm 34:7-8 (ESV)
The angel of the LORD encamps around those who fear him, and delivers them. 8 Oh, taste and see that the LORD is good! Blessed is the man who takes refuge in him!

Exhaustion

I come to you today feeling physically exhausted and weak. I have been working long hours but the challenges are so demanding I don't seem to get ahead and I'm just plain tired. I ask you to help me develop a better schedule where I fulfill the requirements of my job yet allow myself the rest and renewal I need to stay healthy and alert.

1 Peter 4:12-13 (ESV)
Beloved, do not be surprised at the fiery trial when it comes upon you to test you, as though something strange were happening to you. [13] But rejoice insofar as you share Christ's sufferings, that you may also rejoice and be glad when his glory is revealed.

1 Chronicles 16:11 (ESV)
Seek the LORD and his strength; seek his presence continually!

Psalm 55:22 (ESV)
Cast your burden on the LORD, and he will sustain you; he will never permit the righteous to be moved.

Faith

Increase my faith today so your love spills out on everyone I meet. Let the knowledge of you, your love, salvation, and promises radiate from me. Use me and the faith you have given me to touch others in your name. Thank you for the Holy Spirit guiding me and reaching out to others.

Romans 1:17 (ESV)
For in it the righteousness of God is revealed from faith for faith, as it is written, "The righteous shall live by faith."

1 John 4:15-16 (ESV)
Whoever confesses that Jesus is the Son of God, God abides in him, and he in God. 16 So we have come to know and to believe the love that God has for us. God is love, and whoever abides in love abides in God, and God abides in him.

Psalm 136:1 (ESV)
Give thanks to the LORD, for he is good, for his steadfast love endures forever.

Feeling Helpless

I declare my dependence on you. I am unable to stand on my own. Sometimes I feel like a failure because I am so helpless. I want to be strong, be a good model for my students, their families, and for my coworkers. But I struggle to keep my heart pure and my eyes focused on you. Be with me today and let me feel your arms holding me up, then guide my words, my steps and my actions.

Jeremiah 17:14 (ESV)
Heal me, O LORD, and I shall be healed; save me, and I shall be saved, for you are my praise.

John 16:33 (ESV)
I have said these things to you, that in me you may have peace. In the world you will have tribulation. But take heart; I have overcome the world.

Psalm 31:14 (ESV)
But I trust in you, O LORD; I say, "You are my God."

Feeling Inadequate

I look around this building and begin to compare my room to others; my students to others, even my teaching. Sometimes I feel like a failure or at best, inadequate, as I judge myself against these other things. Restore in me a confidence to complete the tasks I have each day to the best of my ability, knowing I have put forth honest effort and sought you as my guide. Give me the energy I need to be the best teacher I can be and do it to your glory.

Hebrews 3:6 (ESV)
but Christ is faithful over God's house as a son. And we are his house if indeed we hold fast our confidence and our boasting in our hope.

Proverbs 23:17-18 (ESV)
Let not your heart envy sinners, but continue in the fear of the LORD all the day. 18 Surely there is a future, and your hope will not be cut off.

Psalm 31:16 (ESV)
Make your face shine on your servant; save me in your steadfast love!

First Day of School

It is a busy season as we prepare for another school year. I ask for strength and health as I organize my thoughts and my room for a new class. Fill me with eagerness and excitement that I might be ready for the task of welcoming new students. Bring children into my room that I can bless and let me be Jesus to them and their families. Grant me unending patience as I pass on your love.

John 8:31-32 (ESV)
So Jesus said to the Jews who had believed him, "If you abide in my word, you are truly my disciples, 32 and you will know the truth, and the truth will set you free."

John 15:9-11 (ESV)
As the Father has loved me, so have I loved you. Abide in my love. 10 If you keep my commandments, you will abide in my love, just as I have kept my Father's commandments and abide in his love. 11 These things I have spoken to you, that my joy may be in you, and that your joy may be full.

Psalm 59:16-17 (ESV)
But I will sing of your strength; I will sing aloud of your steadfast love in the morning. For you have been to me a fortress and a refuge in the day of my distress. 17 O my Strength, I will sing praises to you, for you, O God, are my fortress, the God who shows me steadfast love.

God's Eyes

You see everything through the eyes of love; a compassion that knows no bounds. I want to look at my students and colleagues with that same love and compassion. My families need an extra measure of your love and I want to be available to pass that love on to them. Give me your eyes so my heart will be filled with you and everything I need to love others as you love me. Thank you for your unconditional love.

Hebrews 12:28-29 (ESV)
Therefore let us be grateful for receiving a kingdom that cannot be shaken, and thus let us offer to God acceptable worship, with reverence and awe, 29 for our God is a consuming fire.

Romans 12:12-13 (ESV)
Rejoice in hope, be patient in tribulation, be constant in prayer. 13 Contribute to the needs of the saints and seek to show hospitality.

Psalm 34:18 (ESV)
The LORD is near to the brokenhearted and saves the crushed in spirit.

God's Presence

My room is a busy place. People come and go all day long. I am aware of students talking and working and others entering and engaging with me often. But what I want is the assurance of your presence. When I look out at the sea of students at their desks, I seek to know that you are there as well. Let me see you in their faces and remember to treat them as you would. Stand by me and make my words yours, and my hands, your hands. I need your presence every hour.

Hebrews 13:6 (ESV)
So we can confidently say, "The Lord is my helper; I will not fear; what can man do to me?"

Romans 8:38-39 (ESV)
For I am sure that neither death nor life, nor angels nor rulers, nor things present nor things to come, nor powers, 39 nor height nor depth, nor anything else in all creation, will be able to separate us from the love of God in Christ Jesus our Lord.

Psalm 34:18 (ESV)
The LORD is near to the brokenhearted and saves the crushed in spirit.

Good Health

Almighty God, You are the Great Healer and nothing is impossible with you. Thank you for your daily mercies. Look at this class (or building) and touch everyone who needs healing in their body, soul or spirit. Protect us during this season that illness doesn't get in the way of learning and we stay focused on our purpose here at school. I pray for all the staff and teachers as well. Keep us all well and able to serve you.

2 Timothy 4:18 (ESV)
The Lord will rescue me from every evil deed and bring me safely into his heavenly kingdom. To him be the glory forever and ever. Amen.

2 Corinthians 4:7-9 (ESV)
But we have this treasure in jars of clay, to show that the surpassing power belongs to God and not to us. 8 We are afflicted in every way, but not crushed; perplexed, but not driven to despair; 9 persecuted, but not forsaken; struck down, but not destroyed;

Psalm 29:1-2 (ESV)
Ascribe to the LORD, O heavenly beings, ascribe to the LORD glory and strength. 2 Ascribe to the LORD the glory due his name; worship the LORD in the splendor of holiness.

Good Learning

It is always my intention that all my students will leave each day with their minds and hearts full; eager to return tomorrow curious and ready to learn again. But Lord, often I feel the absence of good learning and I worry that because of many different kinds of distractions, students aren't getting what they need. I pray for a spirit of wonder in this room today; where kids will pay attention, and keep open minds focused on good and appropriate learning.

1 Peter 4:8 (ESV)
Above all, keep loving one another earnestly, since love covers a multitude of sins.

2 Corinthians 4:6-9 (ESV)
For God, who said, "Let light shine out of darkness," has shone in our hearts to give the light of the knowledge of the glory of God in the face of Jesus Christ. 7 But we have this treasure in jars of clay, to show that the surpassing power belongs to God and not to us. 8 We are afflicted in every way, but not crushed; perplexed, but not driven to despair; 9 persecuted, but not forsaken; struck down, but not destroyed.

Psalm 42:5 (ESV)
Why are you cast down, O my soul, and why are you in turmoil within me? Hope in God; for I shall again praise him, my salvation.

Gratefulness

I'm overwhelmed with gratitude. My heart is full to overflowing as I recount what you do in my life and the blessings you give me daily. But your grace is sufficient for me. My true gratefulness begins at the cross with the sacrifice of your Son, Jesus. Thank you for loving me enough to send Him to assure that I will be with you forever in heaven.

John 14:6 (ESV)
Jesus said to him, "I am the way, and the truth, and the life. No one comes to the Father except through me.

1 Peter 5:10-11 (ESV)
And after you have suffered a little while, the God of all grace, who has called you to his eternal glory in Christ, will himself restore, confirm, strengthen, and establish you. 11 To him be the dominion forever and ever. Amen.

Psalm 16:1-2 (ESV)
Preserve me, O God, for in you I take refuge. 2 I say to the LORD, "You are my Lord; I have no good apart from you."

Help Me

I've been tired and busy and I'm overwhelmed with the weight and responsibility of this job. I feel unprepared and not organized for the demands of this day. Go before me, I pray, and remove doubts and hurdles. Prepare my path today and laden it with your grace.

Romans 8:18 (ESV)
For I consider that the sufferings of this present time are not worth comparing with the glory that is to be revealed to us.

2 Corinthians 9:8 (ESV)
And God is able to make all grace abound to you, so that having all sufficiency in all things at all times, you may abound in every good work.

Psalm 34:18 (ESV)
The LORD is near to the brokenhearted and saves the crushed in spirit.

Help Students

There will be students here today who don't know the value or importance of sound learning. Their families don't encourage or support what goes on in school. Change their hearts and turn them so they can see what is good and honorable in your sight.

1 John 1:5-7 (ESV)
This is the message we have heard from him and proclaim to you, that God is light, and in him is no darkness at all. ⁶ If we say we have fellowship with him while we walk in darkness, we lie and do not practice the truth. ⁷ But if we walk in the light, as he is in the light, we have fellowship with one another, and the blood of Jesus his Son cleanses us from all sin.

1 Kings 8:23 (ESV)
"O LORD, God of Israel, there is no God like you, in heaven above or on earth beneath, keeping covenant and showing steadfast love to your servants who walk before you with all their heart;

Psalm 40:3 (ESV)
He put a new song in my mouth, a song of praise to our God. Many will see and fear, and put their trust in the LORD.

His Sufficiency

Almighty God, help me let go of all worldly securities I seek all day long. I acknowledge all I need is you. You have made this promise to me, that your grace is sufficient for me. When all else fails, help me see that I still have the only thing I need for my job and my life. If you are all I have, I have enough.

Isaiah 26:3-4 (ESV)
You keep him in perfect peace whose mind is stayed on you, because he trusts in you. 4 Trust in the LORD forever, for the LORD GOD is an everlasting rock.

2 Corinthians 12:9-10 (ESV)
But he said to me, "My grace is sufficient for you, for my power is made perfect in weakness." Therefore I will boast all the more gladly of my weaknesses, so that the power of Christ may rest upon me. 10 For the sake of Christ, then, I am content with weaknesses, insults, hardships, persecutions, and calamities. For when I am weak, then I am strong.

Psalm 118:5-6 (ESV)
Out of my distress I called on the LORD; the LORD answered me and set me free. 6 The LORD is on my side; I will not fear. What can man do to me?

Hope

You are my only Hope. You alone are faithful and all your promises are true. When the circumstances around me are spinning out of control, you are my Anchor and my trust is in you. Increase my hope today that I am able to be your servant and reflect Jesus to those around me.

1 Timothy 3:16 (ESV)
Great indeed, we confess, is the mystery of godliness: He was manifested in the flesh, vindicated by the Spirit, seen by angels, proclaimed among the nations, believed on in the world, taken up in glory.

2 Peter 1:19 (ESV)
And we have the prophetic word more fully confirmed, to which you will do well to pay attention as to a lamp shining in a dark place, until the day dawns and the morning star rises in your hearts,

Psalm 126:3 (ESV)
The LORD has done great things for us; we are glad.

I Need Armor

No one goes into battle without the proper armor. I enter a battlefield every day, Lord, and need the reassurance your armor gives. Provide for me today and equip me with the protection I need to model what my students need to see. Guide my steps and stay close as I am leading your precious children. I want them to be under your protection too.

Philippians 2:5-8 (ESV)
Have this mind among yourselves, which is yours in Christ Jesus, 6 who, though he was in the form of God, did not count equality with God a thing to be grasped, 7 but emptied himself, by taking the form of a servant, being born in the likeness of men. 8 And being found in human form, he humbled himself by becoming obedient to the point of death, even death on a cross.

Deuteronomy 31:6 (ESV)
Be strong and courageous. Do not fear or be in dread of them, for it is the LORD your God who goes with you. He will not leave you or forsake you."

Psalm 37:23-24 (ESV)
The steps of a man are established by the LORD, when he delights in his way; 24 though he fall, he shall not be cast headlong, for the LORD upholds his hand.

Intercession

I stand in the gap today for all those in my workplace that don't know you. There might be colleagues, families, and students who haven't heard your promises and don't know your love. Put them in my path if I am to be the one to point them to you. Guide my words so they may come to know you and what it means to live a life with the promise of eternal salvation.

Ephesians 4:4-6 (ESV)
There is one body and one Spirit—just as you were called to the one hope that belongs to your call— 5 one Lord, one faith, one baptism, 6 one God and Father of all, who is over all and through all and in all.

Luke 10:27 (ESV)
And he answered, "You shall love the Lord your God with all your heart and with all your soul and with all your strength and with all your mind, and your neighbor as yourself."

Psalm 118:24 (ESV)
This is the day that the LORD has made; let us rejoice and be glad in it.

In the Morning

Soon I will be watching my students walk in the door. Some will come hungry, some sick, and some without a hug this morning. They will come feeling scared, alone, and think they don't belong or fit in. Their clothes may be dirty or they'll need a bath. Let them see your face through me today. Let them feel loved and safe and let them find joy in learning with me today. Help me be what they need. Help me to be Jesus today.

Jeremiah 32:17 (ESV)
'Ah, Lord GOD! It is you who have made the heavens and the earth by your great power and by your outstretched arm! Nothing is too hard for you.

2 Corinthians 4:16 (ESV)
So we do not lose heart. Though our outer self is wasting away, our inner self is being renewed day by day.

Psalm 5:12 (ESV)
For you bless the righteous, O LORD; you cover him with favor as with a shield.

Joy

Nothing in this world brings me the everlasting joy I find in knowing Jesus is my Savior. When everything in my day threatens to turn me away from you, make my path straight and my eyes focused on the cross. It is because of that cross I feel joy; a joy that is ever-present and always available. Make that joy real to me today and dispel all worldly thoughts that deceive me.

1 Timothy 6:6-8 (ESV)
But godliness with contentment is great gain, 7 for we brought nothing into the world, and we cannot take anything out of the world. 8 But if we have food and clothing, with these we will be content.

James 1:2-4 (ESV)
Count it all joy, my brothers, when you meet trials of various kinds, 3 for you know that the testing of your faith produces steadfastness. 4 And let steadfastness have its full effect, that you may be perfect and complete, lacking in nothing.

Psalm 130:5-6 (ESV)
I wait for the LORD, my soul waits, and in his word I hope; 6 my soul waits for the Lord more than watchmen for the morning, more than watchmen for the morning.

Lift a Burden Today

God of Mercy, my heart is heavy and while I know you are with me, I need to feel your presence today. I want my focus to be you, not my heavy heart. Lift my spirit and turn my eyes to you, the One who can change my sorrow into joy. Show me the path to the cross that I may lay my burden at your feet. I submit to your will and ask for your comfort.

Jeremiah 29:13 (ESV)
You will seek me and find me, when you seek me with all your heart.

Exodus 14:14 (ESV)
The LORD will fight for you, and you have only to be silent."

Psalm 95:1-4 (ESV)
Oh come, let us sing to the LORD; let us make a joyful noise to the rock of our salvation! ² Let us come into his presence with thanksgiving; let us make a joyful noise to him with songs of praise! ³ For the LORD is a great God, and a great King above all gods. ⁴ In his hand are the depths of the earth; the heights of the mountains are his also.

Lighten My Load

Lord, I feel the weight of my responsibilities today. Help me look to the cross and lay those burdens at your feet. It is not your desire that I walk alone today feeling afraid or weary. Help me let go of everything that is not of you. Empty me and let me walk away filled with the power of the Holy Spirit so your light is what people see and your love is what they feel.

Proverbs 15:15 (ESV)
All the days of the afflicted are evil, but the cheerful of heart has a continual feast.

Galatians 2:20 (ESV)
I have been crucified with Christ. It is no longer I who live, but Christ who lives in me. And the life I now live in the flesh I live by faith in the Son of God, who loved me and gave himself for me.

Psalm 20:7 (ESV)
Some trust in chariots and some in horses, but we trust in the name of the LORD our God.

Listen to Him

Lord, there are sounds and confusion around me all day. I seek a time where you become my refuge and I can hear your voice. Quiet my heart and mind so that even in the busy-ness of my day, I can hear what you are saying. Grant me discernment so I can follow your direction, and place in my heart the assurance that you are with me in everything I do.

Romans 8:6 (ESV)
For to set the mind on the flesh is death, but to set the mind on the Spirit is life and peace.

Isaiah 30:18 (ESV)
Therefore the LORD waits to be gracious to you, and therefore he exalts himself to show mercy to you. For the LORD is a God of justice; blessed are all those who wait for him.

Psalm 147:11 (ESV)
but the LORD takes pleasure in those who fear him, in those who hope in his steadfast love.

Living Your Word

Your Word is life to me. You are sovereign, faithful, and perfect in your wisdom and unconditional love. Give me an understanding of Scripture so I can be an example to my students of what you want your people to be. I seek your face daily and want to be obedient to what your Word says to me. Let your Word be my guide.

Hebrews 4:12-13 (ESV)
For the word of God is living and active, sharper than any two-edged sword, piercing to the division of soul and of spirit, of joints and of marrow, and discerning the thoughts and intentions of the heart. [13] And no creature is hidden from his sight, but all are naked and exposed to the eyes of him to whom we must give account.

Ephesians 1:17 (ESV)
... that the God of our Lord Jesus Christ, the Father of glory, may give you the Spirit of wisdom and of revelation in the knowledge of him,

Psalm 139:1-4 (ESV)
O LORD, you have searched me and known me! [2] You know when I sit down and when I rise up; you discern my thoughts from afar. [3] You search out my path and my lying down and are acquainted with all my ways. [4] Even before a word is on my tongue, behold, O LORD, you know it altogether.

Look for Blessings

My days are so busy. Sometimes they fly by on autopilot. Other days seem slow and tedious. But in all circumstances and challenges, I ask that you reveal to me the good that I can do and the blessing that you intended for me and others around me. Every day is a blessing in itself and I am grateful for each one. Give me a vision today of how I can be Jesus and bless those around me. You are the Giver of All Good. Thank you for today and all that will come my way.

2 Corinthians 9:15 (ESV)
Thanks be to God for his inexpressible gift!

Isaiah 43:18-19 (ESV)
"Remember not the former things, nor consider the things of old. 19 Behold, I am doing a new thing; now it springs forth, do you not perceive it? I will make a way in the wilderness and rivers in the desert.

Psalm 149:4 (ESV)
For the LORD takes pleasure in his people; he adorns the humble with salvation.

Love

You love me with a perfect love; unlike anyone on earth can. When I feel unloved today, assure me that the only love that really matters surrounds me and protects me, driving out fear. Give me an abundance of love so it spills out of me and touches everyone in my path. I pray that everyone will see Jesus in that love and they are drawn closer to you as they are touched. Thank you for filling my heart to overflowing.

Hebrews 13:8 (ESV)
Jesus Christ is the same yesterday and today and forever.

Matthew 5:14-16 (NKJV)
You are the light of the world. A city that is set on a hill cannot be hidden. 15 Nor do they light a lamp and put it under a basket, but on a lampstand, and it gives light to all who are in the house. 16 Let your light so shine before men, that they may see your good works and glorify your Father in heaven.

Psalm 107:1 (ESV)
Oh give thanks to the LORD, for he is good, for his steadfast love endures forever!

Mercy

Your mercies are new every morning and available to me no matter what I have done. You withhold the punishment I deserve and give me the love and mercy I don't deserve. Thank you for that blessing. Give me the power to pass that same mercy on to students in my school and all those working around me. Be my focus and the Spirit that guides and sustains me all day.

Lamentations 3:22-23 (ESV)
The steadfast love of the LORD never ceases; his mercies never come to an end; 23 they are new every morning; great is your faithfulness.

Isaiah 44:22 (ESV)
I have blotted out your transgressions like a cloud and your sins like mist; return to me, for I have redeemed you.

Colossians 3:12-14 (ESV)
Put on then, as God's chosen ones, holy and beloved, compassionate hearts, kindness, humility, meekness, and patience, 13 bearing with one another and, if one has a complaint against another, forgiving each other; as the Lord has forgiven you, so you also must forgive. 14 And above all these put on love, which binds everything together in perfect harmony.

Psalm 13:5 (ESV)
But I have trusted in your steadfast love; my heart shall rejoice in your salvation.

Mercy and Grace

I know I don't deserve the mercy and grace you give so freely. But I need your gift every day. I ask for a portion of your unfailing grace that I may be able to pass it on to students and colleagues alike. You are the Source and Giver of all things good and I am bold to ask for your favor today.

Hebrews 11:1 (ESV)
Now faith is the assurance of things hoped for, the conviction of things not seen.

Philippians 4:4-5 (ESV)
Rejoice in the Lord always; again I will say, rejoice. 5 Let your reasonableness be known to everyone. The Lord is at hand;

Psalm 118:5-6 (ESV)
Out of my distress I called on the LORD; the LORD answered me and set me free. 6 The LORD is on my side; I will not fear. What can man do to me?

Miracle Needed

You have all the power and perfect wisdom. I rely on you and your strength today. The circumstances seem impossible and I feel inadequate and helpless. So, I ask for nothing short of a miracle and surrender this burden to you. I cast my cares on you, Lord, and trust that your perfect will be done.

Philippians 3:12-14 (ESV)
Not that I have already obtained this or am already perfect, but I press on to make it my own, because Christ Jesus has made me his own. [13] Brothers, I do not consider that I have made it my own. But one thing I do: forgetting what lies behind and straining forward to what lies ahead, [14] I press on toward the goal for the prize of the upward call of God in Christ Jesus.

Philippians 3:20-21 (ESV)
But our citizenship is in heaven, and from it we await a Savior, the Lord Jesus Christ, [21] who will transform our lowly body to be like his glorious body, by the power that enables him even to subject all things to himself.

Psalm 68:19 (ESV)
Blessed be the Lord, who daily bears us up; God is our salvation. Selah

Model for Colleagues or Student Teacher

God, you are the Master Teacher; perfect in wisdom and your Son was the Model, sent for us. Today, as I model good teaching for (name) I want to reflect only the best; best effort, perfect calm, assurance, and a Godly spirit. Keep your arms around me today and let me feel your presence as I seek to reflect what you have made me to be. My trust is in you.

Hebrews 10:12-14 (ESV)
But when Christ had offered for all time a single sacrifice for sins, he sat down at the right hand of God, 13 waiting from that time until his enemies should be made a footstool for his feet. 14 For by a single offering he has perfected for all time those who are being sanctified.

Zephaniah 3:17 (ESV)
The LORD your God is in your midst, a mighty one who will save; he will rejoice over you with gladness; he will quiet you by his love; he will exult over you with loud singing.

Psalm 33:20-22 (ESV)
20 Our soul waits for the LORD; he is our help and our shield. 21 For our heart is glad in him, because we trust in his holy name. 22 Let your steadfast love, O LORD, be upon us, even as we hope in you.

My Families

Lord, You are the Creator of All Good Things and you provide for our needs. I have families represented in my room where there is great need. You know all their circumstances and the desires of their hearts. I ask you for mercy for those families where good hard labor is modeled and yet, it isn't enough to feed everyone. Many moms and dads face unemployment and their families are suffering because of it. Reward honesty and integrity with your bounty, Lord, that all will work for their good and your glory.

Proverbs 4:18 (ESV)
But the path of the righteous is like the light of dawn, which shines brighter and brighter until full day.

Luke 12:22-24 (ESV)
And he said to his disciples, "Therefore I tell you, do not be anxious about your life, what you will eat, nor about your body, what you will put on. 23 For life is more than food, and the body more than clothing. 24 Consider the ravens: they neither sow nor reap, they have neither storehouse nor barn, and yet God feeds them. Of how much more value are you than the birds!

Psalm 37:4 (ESV)
Delight yourself in the LORD, and he will give you the desires of your heart.

My Family

Heavenly Father, I get consumed with all the burdens and responsibilities of this job and sometimes I neglect my own family at home. I pray for their safety and protection today and a growing love for you. Draw them to you that everything they do today will be for their good and your glory. You love them even more than I do and I know you will be with them today when I can't. Give us all your blessing today, Lord, and protect us from the evil one.

John 10:14-15 (ESV)
I am the good shepherd. I know my own and my own know me, 15 just as the Father knows me and I know the Father; and I lay down my life for the sheep.

Proverbs 3:5-6 (ESV)
Trust in the LORD with all your heart, and do not lean on your own understanding. 6 In all your ways acknowledge him, and he will make straight your paths.

Psalm 139:1-4 (ESV)
O LORD, you have searched me and known me! 2 You know when I sit down and when I rise up; you discern my thoughts from afar. 3 You search out my path and my lying down and are acquainted with all my ways. 4 Even before a word is on my tongue, behold, O LORD, you know it altogether.

My Heart

Guard my heart today, Lord. Empty me of everything that is not from you. Fill it with love and kindness; the kind that can only come from you. Let my full heart overflow, spilling on others that they may see you and acknowledge your power and greatness. To you be the honor and glory, Lord, today, and always.

Philippians 1:6 (ESV)
And I am sure of this, that he who began a good work in you will bring it to completion at the day of Jesus Christ.

2 Corinthians 2:14 (ESV)
But thanks be to God, who in Christ always leads us in triumphal procession, and through us spreads the fragrance of the knowledge of him everywhere.

Psalm 39:7-8 (ESV)
"And now, O Lord, for what do I wait? My hope is in you. 8 Deliver me from all my transgressions. Do not make me the scorn of the fool!

My Principal

Lord, my principal, _____, works hard every day and I'm asking you for special favor. The days grow long and the work is never done and yet, s/he perseveres. Allow time for rest and renewal and keep her/him healthy. Lift her/him during the times in the day when s/he needs to be bold, patient, firm, or tender. Give her/him discernment as there are so many decisions to be made all day long. Let her/him be a model of your love and reflect the face of Jesus to everyone in our building.

Proverbs 16:3 (ESV)
Commit your work to the LORD, and your plans will be established.

Isaiah 40:30-31 (ESV)
Even youths shall faint and be weary, and young men shall fall exhausted; 31 but they who wait for the LORD shall renew their strength; they shall mount up with wings like eagles; they shall run and not be weary; they shall walk and not faint.

Psalm 19:1-2 (ESV)
The heavens declare the glory of God, and the sky above proclaims his handiwork. 2 Day to day pours out speech, and night to night reveals knowledge.

Observation Today

I am going to be observed today. I will rely on you and your presence in my room to calm my thoughts, keep me focused, and with you by my side, I will use your confidence to teach my lesson with clarity. I pray for an extra measure of patience and understanding for (the person doing the observing) as s/he watches me with my students today. I surrender this time to you.

Ecclesiastes 3:1 (ESV)
For everything there is a season, and a time for every matter under heaven:

Philippians 4:19 (ESV)
And my God will supply every need of yours according to his riches in glory in Christ Jesus.

Psalm 61:1-4 (ESV)
Hear my cry, O God, listen to my prayer; 2 from the end of the earth I call to you when my heart is faint. Lead me to the rock that is higher than I, 3 for you have been my refuge, a strong tower against the enemy. 4 Let me dwell in your tent forever! Let me take refuge under the shelter of your wings! Selah

Open My Hands

Lord, sometimes I go through my day so busy working and focused on tasks and accomplishments, that I don't realize my eyes are closed to your work around me and my hands are not open. With closed hands, I can neither serve nor be served. I cannot hold the hands of my students nor can I grab on to yours. Keep my hands open, Lord, so I can keep all of us connected to you.

Romans 8:26-27 (ESV)
Likewise the Spirit helps us in our weakness. For we do not know what to pray for as we ought, but the Spirit himself intercedes for us with groanings too deep for words. 27 And he who searches hearts knows what is the mind of the Spirit, because the Spirit intercedes for the saints according to the will of God.

John 15:5 (ESV)
I am the vine; you are the branches. Whoever abides in me and I in him, he it is that bears much fruit, for apart from me you can do nothing.

Psalm 16:11 (ESV)
You make known to me the path of life; in your presence there is fullness of joy; at your right hand are pleasures forevermore.

Open My Heart

Open my heart, Lord, to hear what you want me to know today. Help me hear your words, feeling your arm to either nudge me or hold me. Make your will known to me that everything I do and say comes from you. I want others to be blessed by knowing you through me. Use me in my classroom, my school, and my home; to those I know and those I meet.

Colossians 4:2 (ESV)
Continue steadfastly in prayer, being watchful in it with thanksgiving.

Romans 12:10-12 (ESV)
Love one another with brotherly affection. Outdo one another in showing honor. [11] Do not be slothful in zeal, be fervent in spirit, serve the Lord. [12] Rejoice in hope, be patient in tribulation, be constant in prayer.

Psalm 37:4 (ESV)
Delight yourself in the LORD, and he will give you the desires of your heart.

Parent Blessing

You are the giver of all good things and you know what is good for us. I beseech you to look at the parents of the students in this room (building) and have mercy on them. Give them your grace. Lead them in the wisdom and knowledge they need to be the kind of parents you want them to be.

Hebrews 11:6 (ESV)
And without faith it is impossible to please him, for whoever would draw near to God must believe that he exists and that he rewards those who seek him.

Ephesians 4:29 (ESV)
Let no corrupting talk come out of your mouths, but only such as is good for building up, as fits the occasion, that it may give grace to those who hear.

Psalm 86:11 (ESV)
Teach me your way, O LORD, that I may walk in your truth; unite my heart to fear your name.

Parents

You are the Perfect Father. You love us more than any earthly parent and you do it unconditionally. You extend forgiveness and mercy where we don't deserve it. Please look at the parents of these families and bless them as only you can. Protect them and give them what they need to be more like you.

Daniel 12:3 (ESV)
And those who are wise shall shine like the brightness of the sky above; and those who turn many to righteousness, like the stars forever and ever.

1 John 3:1 (ESV)
See what kind of love the Father has given to us, that we should be called children of God; and so we are. The reason why the world does not know us is that it did not know him.

Psalm 9:10 (ESV)
And those who know your name put their trust in you, for you, O LORD, have not forsaken those who seek you.

Parent Teacher Conferences

Lord, I'm going to be meeting with parents today. I pray their hearts and minds will be open to what I have to share with them and they will know I love their child and want only what's good for them. Give me words of truth that you will be given the glory.

Philippians 2:9-11 (ESV)
Therefore God has highly exalted him and bestowed on him the name that is above every name, 10 so that at the name of Jesus every knee should bow, in heaven and on earth and under the earth, 11 and every tongue confess that Jesus Christ is Lord, to the glory of God the Father.

Philippians 4:13 (ESV)
I can do all things through him who strengthens me.

Psalm 71:20-21 (ESV)
You who have made me see many troubles and calamities will revive me again; from the depths of the earth you will bring me up again. 21 You will increase my greatness and comfort me again.

Patience

Lord, grant me the character of Christ. Give me the patience he had on this earth; not a tolerance for evil but a Godly patience to wait on you for the right time, the right words, and actions. Fill my heart with a righteous attitude that I may model Jesus today.

2 Timothy 4:8 (NKJV)
Finally, there is laid up for me the crown of righteousness, which the Lord, the righteous Judge, will give to me on that Day, and not to me only but also to all who have loved His appearing.

Luke 6:37-38 (ESV)
"Judge not, and you will not be judged; condemn not, and you will not be condemned; forgive, and you will be forgiven; 38 give, and it will be given to you. Good measure, pressed down, shaken together, running over, will be put into your lap. For with the measure you use it will be measured back to you."

Psalm 32:7 (ESV)
You are a hiding place for me; you preserve me from trouble; you surround me with shouts of deliverance. Selah

Patience II

I thank you for every hour of this day and I pray that somewhere in every hour I will see your face. Right now I am feeling impatient and anxious and I want what I do and say to glorify you. So, I ask that you replace the impatience with your strength and patience; that I can surrender all these imperfect feelings to you and you will grant me calm and serenity that only you can give. I ask it in the precious name of your Son, Jesus.

Hebrews 12:11 (NRSV)
Now, discipline always seems painful rather than pleasant at the time, but later it yields the peaceful fruit of righteousness to those who have been trained by it.

1 Thessalonians 5:16-18 (ESV)
Rejoice always, 17 pray without ceasing, 18 give thanks in all circumstances; for this is the will of God in Christ Jesus for you.

Psalm 119:35 (ESV)
Lead me in the path of your commandments, for I delight in it.

Peace

In my whole day at school, there is very little peace. My students are busy or loud, distracted or seeking attention. In all of this, there is little peace. Pour your Spirit of peace throughout our room today and cause minds and hearts to be stilled and calm that good learning will happen. Increase in them the ability to be kind, attentive, accepting and caring about each other; that we might foster a community where peace will grow.

Hebrews 4:16 (NKJV)
Let us therefore come boldly to the throne of grace, that we may obtain mercy and find grace to help in time of need.

Galatians 6:9-10 (NKJV)
And let us not grow weary while doing good, for in due season we shall reap if we do not lose heart. [10] Therefore, as we have opportunity, let us do good to all, especially to those who are of the household of faith.

Psalm 46:10 (ESV)
"Be still, and know that I am God. I will be exalted among the nations, I will be exalted in the earth!"

Peace II

Sometimes I feel as if all I do is stifle arguments and smooth out the unrest that occurs between students. It disrupts our learning and creates an unpleasant atmosphere in my room and in our school. It feels like Satan gets a foothold whenever conflict breaks out. I want your Spirit to prevail in this building. Calm hearts, hold tongues, teach compassion and understanding so my students aren't acting out in anger and bitterness. Help me model Jesus and the wisdom and peace He shows. Grant us your peace.

Matthew 7:24 (ESV)
"Everyone then who hears these words of mine and does them will be like a wise man who built his house on the rock.

Proverbs 17:22 (ESV)
A joyful heart is good medicine, but a crushed spirit dries up the bones.

Psalm 63:1-4 (ESV)
O God, you are my God; earnestly I seek you; my soul thirsts for you; my flesh faints for you, as in a dry and weary land where there is no water. 2 So I have looked upon you in the sanctuary, beholding your power and glory. 3 Because your steadfast love is better than life, my lips will praise you. 4 So I will bless you as long as I live; in your name I will lift up my hands.

Peace in the Classroom

Lord, bring peace to this classroom. When comments are made, let no one take offense. Help us stay focused on learning and extend grace and mercy every hour.

Proverbs 16:24 (ESV)
Gracious words are like a honeycomb, sweetness to the soul and health to the body.

2 Samuel 22:33 (NKJV)
God is my strength and power, And He makes my way perfect.

Psalm 5:11-12 (NKJV)
But let all those rejoice who put their trust in You; Let them ever shout for joy, because You defend them; Let those also who love Your name Be joyful in You. 12 For You, O LORD, will bless the righteous; With favor You will surround him as with a shield.

Phone Calls Home

I have a list of names that require parental contact today. Most of what I have to say will be interpreted as negative and could be cause for parents to act defensively. Help me choose my words carefully, Lord, so I can deliver the message in the spirit it is intended so the responses will be supportive and help make positive changes in learning or behavior.

Colossians 2:2-3 (ESV)
that their hearts may be encouraged, being knit together in love, to reach all the riches of full assurance of understanding and the knowledge of God's mystery, which is Christ, 3 in whom are hidden all the treasures of wisdom and knowledge.

Isaiah 58:11 (ESV)
And the LORD will guide you continually and satisfy your desire in scorched places and make your bones strong; and you shall be like a watered garden, like a spring of water, whose waters do not fail.

Psalm 8:1-4 (ESV) 1
O LORD, our Lord, how majestic is your name in all the earth! You have set your glory above the heavens. 2 Out of the mouth of babies and infants, you have established strength because of your foes, to still the enemy and the avenger. 3 When I look at your heavens, the work of your fingers, the moon and the stars, which you have set in place, 4 what is man that you are mindful of him, and the son of man that you care for him?

Pleasing Him

All day long I try to keep a balance in my classroom where students will listen and learn in a calm environment. I feel like I'm always trying to please them or my principal. What I want is to please you. It is you I serve and from you come all my gifts. I couldn't do this job if you didn't gift me for it. Keep my mind on you today, Lord, working so whatever I do pleases you.

Deuteronomy 6:13 (ESV)
It is the LORD your God you shall fear. Him you shall serve and by his name you shall swear

Colossians 3:17 (ESV)
And whatever you do, in word or deed, do everything in the name of the Lord Jesus, giving thanks to God the Father through him.

Psalm 43:4 (NKJV)
Then I will go to the altar of God, To God my exceeding joy; And on the harp I will praise You, O God, my God.

Praise

You alone are worthy of my praise, Lord, and my prayer is that I praise you today with everything I say and do. Let every word bring you honor and may my actions reflect your goodness and love. Remind me every moment that you are the source of everything good in my life; that you alone are in control. Bring that control into my classroom that you will receive everything we do today as praise; praise for who you are; a mighty, perfect, all-wise Father.

Philippians 4:9 (ESV)
What you have learned and received and heard and seen in me—practice these things, and the God of peace will be with you.

James 4:6-8 (ESV)
But he gives more grace. Therefore it says, "God opposes the proud, but gives grace to the humble." 7 Submit yourselves therefore to God. Resist the devil, and he will flee from you. 8 Draw near to God, and he will draw near to you. Cleanse your hands, you sinners, and purify your hearts, you double-minded.

Psalm 27:7-8 (ESV)
Hear, O LORD, when I cry aloud; be gracious to me and answer me! 8 You have said, "Seek my face." My heart says to you, "Your face, LORD, do I seek."

Prayer of Jabez

Just as you heard Jabez asking you to increase his territory, I ask you to increase mine. Show me where you are working so I may join you and follow. Give me boldness so I can share who you are and where my strength comes from, then others may know you and follow as well. Let me see you in my work today and bless those I can reach.

Jeremiah 29:11-12 (ESV)
For I know the plans I have for you, declares the LORD, plans for welfare and not for evil, to give you a future and a hope. 12 Then you will call upon me and come and pray to me, and I will hear you.

Acts 4:12 (ESV)
And there is salvation in no one else, for there is no other name under heaven given among men by which we must be saved."

Psalm 56:3-4 (ESV)
When I am afraid, I put my trust in you. 4 In God, whose word I praise, in God I trust; I shall not be afraid. What can flesh do to me?

Protection at Recess

My students struggle with social skills and showing kindness during their free time. Help them feel accepted and show acceptance. Help them feel loved and show love. Help them grow in the relationships they're forming during this recreation that they may learn to reflect your goodness and kindness.

Romans 8:28 (ESV)
And we know that for those who love God all things work together for good, for those who are called according to his purpose.

Nahum 1:7 (ESV)
The LORD is good, a stronghold in the day of trouble; he knows those who take refuge in him.

Psalm 84:11-12 (ESV)
For the LORD God is a sun and shield; the LORD bestows favor and honor. No good thing does he withhold from those who walk uprightly. [12] O LORD of hosts, blessed is the one who trusts in you!

Protection for Families

My students and their families need your protection. Put a hedge around each one that the enemy would have no power over them. Protect me as I seek to be Jesus in this school today.

Hebrews 12:1-3 (ESV)
¹Therefore, since we are surrounded by so great a cloud of witnesses, let us also lay aside every weight, and sin which clings so closely, and let us run with endurance the race that is set before us, ² looking to Jesus, the founder and perfecter of our faith, who for the joy that was set before him endured the cross, despising the shame, and is seated at the right hand of the throne of God. ³ Consider him who endured from sinners such hostility against himself, so that you may not grow weary or fainthearted.

John 16:22 (ESV)
So also you have sorrow now, but I will see you again, and your hearts will rejoice, and no one will take your joy from you.

Psalm 32:10 (ESV)
Many are the sorrows of the wicked, but steadfast love surrounds the one who trusts in the LORD.

Protection for the Building

Lord, sometimes it feels as if our building is under spiritual attack. There is chaos, frustration, adversity, and tension everywhere. Dispel everything that is not of you, Lord, and I pray Satan will be bound and have no control in this building. Let your Spirit prevail and restore us to your peace with a hedge of protection at every corner. Reclaim this building for good and not for evil.

Colossians 1:16-17 (ESV)
For by him all things were created, in heaven and on earth, visible and invisible, whether thrones or dominions or rulers or authorities—all things were created through him and for him. [17] And he is before all things, and in him all things hold together.

1 Corinthians 15:57 (ESV)
But thanks be to God, who gives us the victory through our Lord Jesus Christ.

Psalm 18:27-28 (ESV)
For you save a humble people, but the haughty eyes you bring down. [28] For it is you who light my lamp; the LORD my God lightens my darkness.

Protection from Outside Influences

I lift up my students and all others in the building today. There is much in this world to be feared but not if we have your armor. Ward off evil in their hearts; fear or sadness. Let this room and this building serve as a haven that is guarded by your angels on every side. Let no harm come to all who enter today.

Deuteronomy 23:14 (ESV)
Because the LORD your God walks in the midst of your camp, to deliver you and to give up your enemies before you, therefore your camp must be holy, so that he may not see anything indecent among you and turn away from you.

Matthew 7:7 (ESV)
"Ask, and it will be given to you; seek, and you will find; knock, and it will be opened to you.

Psalm 40:11 (ESV)
As for you, O LORD, you will not restrain your mercy from me; your steadfast love and your faithfulness will ever preserve me!

Public Presentation

You are the Master of Communication. You can calm storms and restore peace with just a word. I ask for an extra measure of your wisdom today as I make a public presentation. Help me organize my thoughts, clear my head and remove any hesitation and lack of confidence I may feel. Let me feel your arms around me as I stand there knowing that you are with me. Make my message clear and touch the listeners that they will be fed with good and helpful information. I want to be a blessing today.

Matthew 10:29-31 (ESV)
Are not two sparrows sold for a penny? And not one of them will fall to the ground apart from your Father. 30 But even the hairs of your head are all numbered. 31 Fear not, therefore; you are of more value than many sparrows.

Micah 7:7-8 (ESV)
But as for me, I will look to the LORD; I will wait for the God of my salvation; my God will hear me. 8 Rejoice not over me, O my enemy; when I fall, I shall rise; when I sit in darkness, the LORD will be a light to me.

Psalm 94:19 (ESV)
When the cares of my heart are many, your consolations cheer my soul.

Renewal

It was a long day, Lord, and I'm tired. I saw lots of hurt, frustration, and anger today. I pray that, now, at the end of this day, these feelings will all be washed away and be replaced with your understanding, patience, and love; that tomorrow when all my students return, they will have a renewed sense of hope and a genuine desire to learn. Don't let dissension fill our halls and rooms but let your peace prevail.

John 7:37-38 (ESV)
On the last day of the feast, the great day, Jesus stood up and cried out, "If anyone thirsts, let him come to me and drink. 38 Whoever believes in me, as the Scripture has said, 'Out of his heart will flow rivers of living water.'"

Ephesians 4:31-32 (ESV)
Let all bitterness and wrath and anger and clamor and slander be put away from you, along with all malice. 32 Be kind to one another, tenderhearted, forgiving one another, as God in Christ forgave you.

Psalm 6:4 (ESV)
Turn, O LORD, deliver my life; save me for the sake of your steadfast love.

Renew My Mind

My mind gets full and cluttered. My schedule is busy and crowded. Renew my mind, organize my thoughts, and make room for the words that are most important to me. Bring the verses to my mind that I need for each day knowing that your instruction is all I need. Let your words be the words that start my day and uphold me as I teach. I rely on this gift to provide the strength my mind needs all day.

Romans 12:2 (ESV)
Do not be conformed to this world, but be transformed by the renewal of your mind, that by testing you may discern what is the will of God, what is good and acceptable and perfect.

Ephesians 1:3-8 (ESV)
Blessed be the God and Father of our Lord Jesus Christ, who has blessed us in Christ with every spiritual blessing in the heavenly places, 4 even as he chose us in him before the foundation of the world, that we should be holy and blameless before him. In love 5 he predestined us for adoption as sons through Jesus Christ, according to the purpose of his will, 6 to the praise of his glorious grace, with which he has blessed us in the Beloved. 7 In him we have redemption through his blood, the forgiveness of our trespasses, according to the riches of his grace, 8 which he lavished upon us, in all wisdom and insight

Psalm 119:105 (ASV)
Thy word is a lamp unto my feet, And light unto my path.

Report Cards

I'm swamped with paper work and deadlines and I'm feeling overwhelmed. Sometimes the responsibilities of teaching are exhausting. This week I have to fill out report cards for all my students. I want to be fair and report truth. Please go before me and clear the path so when I begin writing about my students I am clear and honest. Keep me focused and give me the energy I need to finish well.

Romans 12:12 (ESV)
Rejoice in hope, be patient in tribulation, be constant in prayer.

2 Corinthians 4:17-18 (ESV)
For this light momentary affliction is preparing for us an eternal weight of glory beyond all comparison, [18] as we look not to the things that are seen but to the things that are unseen. For the things that are seen are transient, but the things that are unseen are eternal.

Psalm 5:3 (NRSV)
O LORD, in the morning you hear my voice; in the morning I plead my case to you, and watch.

Salt and Light

As your children, you have called us to be the salt and light on this earth. As salt, we change the flavor of our environment and demonstrate Christ-like love for those around us. As light, we show the world what it means to live like Christ and point to the One True Light. Sometimes I don't feel like loving all those around me or even living like Christ wants me to. Change my heart that I might let the Holy Spirit guide my words and actions today and be worthy to be called your child.

1 Peter 2:9 (NRSV)
But you are a chosen race, a royal priesthood, a holy nation, God's own people, in order that you may proclaim the mighty acts of him who called you out of darkness into his marvelous light.

Proverbs 17:27 (NKJV)
He who has knowledge spares his words, And a man of understanding is of a calm spirit.

Psalm 145:10 (ESV)
All your works shall give thanks to you, O LORD, and all your saints shall bless you!

Seek Truth

The world influences my class and me all day long. Things get muddied and unclear. Work in this classroom so your truth would prevail. Help my students understand the importance of knowing and accepting truth and teach them how to speak it.

Matthew 6:33 (ESV)
But seek first the kingdom of God and his righteousness, and all these things will be added to you.

Micah 6:8 (ESV)
He has told you, O man, what is good; and what does the LORD require of you but to do justice, and to love kindness, and to walk humbly with your God?

Psalm 86:4 (ESV)
Gladden the soul of your servant, for to you, O Lord, do I lift up my soul.

Self-Control

I alone create the environment in my classroom. If I escalate, my students will too. Give me the self-control to remain a calm model for them just as Christ is a model for me. I look to you and your mercy to grant me what I need for this day. I lack the power to do this on my own and rely on you to make me the servant you want me to be today.

1 Peter 1:13 (NRSV)
Therefore prepare your minds for action; discipline yourselves; set all your hope on the grace that Jesus Christ will bring you when he is revealed.

Galatians 5:22-23 (ESV)
But the fruit of the Spirit is love, joy, peace, patience, kindness, goodness, faithfulness, 23 gentleness, self-control; against such things there is no law.

Psalm 16:11 (NRSV)
You show me the path of life. In your presence there is fullness of joy; in your right hand are pleasures forevermore.

Serve You

You've given us all a prescribed number of hours each day where we can choose how best to serve you. Make me wise in my use of time today. I surrender my schedule to you and thank you for your direction.

Colossians 1:10-12 (ESV)
¹ so as to walk in a manner worthy of the Lord, fully pleasing to him, bearing fruit in every good work and increasing in the knowledge of God. ¹¹ May you be strengthened with all power, according to his glorious might, for all endurance and patience with joy, ¹² giving thanks to the Father, who has qualified you to share in the inheritance of the saints in light.

Colossians 3:23-24 (ESV)
Whatever you do, work heartily, as for the Lord and not for men, ²⁴ knowing that from the Lord you will receive the inheritance as your reward. You are serving the Lord Christ.

Psalm 130:5-6 (ESV)
I wait for the LORD, my soul waits, and in his word I hope; ⁶ my soul waits for the Lord more than watchmen for the morning, more than watchmen for the morning.

Stay with Me

My prayer today is that you make your presence known to me so I am reminded every minute that you are with me. I need the assurance that you are standing next to me while I teach, that you are there in every word of instruction and with every decision I make. Help me treat my students with the same love and support I am asking you for. Give them your love through me.

Matthew 5:3 (ESV)
"Blessed are the poor in spirit, for theirs is the kingdom of heaven.

Isaiah 54:10 (ESV)
For the mountains may depart and the hills be removed, but my steadfast love shall not depart from you, and my covenant of peace shall not be removed," says the LORD, who has compassion on you.

Psalm 19:14 (ESV)
Let the words of my mouth and the meditation of my heart be acceptable in your sight, O LORD, my rock and my redeemer.

Student's Last Day at School

Today is (name)'s last day at our school. As he/she leaves, let him/her feel loved by us but excited about a new classroom. Go with him/her to the new school and provide protection from anxiety, worry or any harm. Keep your arms of comfort around him/her and fill him/her with your peace. Bring new friends his/her way and bless his/her family as they get settled in their new home. It is in Jesus' perfect name I put my trust.

Hebrews 7:25-26 (ESV)
Consequently, he is able to save to the uttermost those who draw near to God through him, since he always lives to make intercession for them. [26] For it was indeed fitting that we should have such a high priest, holy, innocent, unstained, separated from sinners, and exalted above the heavens.

Deuteronomy 31:8 (ESV)
It is the LORD who goes before you. He will be with you; he will not leave you or forsake you. Do not fear or be dismayed."

Psalm 91:1-4 (ESV)
[1] He who dwells in the shelter of the Most High will abide in the shadow of the Almighty.
[2] I will say to the LORD, "My refuge and my fortress, my God, in whom I trust." [3] For he will deliver you from the snare of the fowler and from the deadly pestilence. [4] He will cover you with his pinions, and under his wings you will find refuge; his faithfulness is a shield and buckler.

Summer Vacation

Heavenly Father, excitement and apprehension fill the air at school as we prepare to say good bye to classmates and teachers and begin our summer break. Surround these students and protect them in the coming months as they enjoy a vacation from school. Keep them safe and help them find wholesome activities to occupy their time. Bless the time they spend with family and friends and always direct their thoughts toward you. Nourish them in body and mind until they are ready to return to school next fall.

Psalm 18:35 (ESV)
You have given me the shield of your salvation, and your right hand supported me, and your gentleness made me great.

Proverbs 4:11-12 (ESV)
I have taught you the way of wisdom; I have led you in the paths of uprightness. 12 When you walk, your step will not be hampered, and if you run, you will not stumble.

Psalm 3:5-6 (ESV)
I lay down and slept; I woke again, for the LORD sustained me. 6 I will not be afraid of many thousands of people who have set themselves against me all around.

Surrender

While I command and control this classroom, I want to be purposeful in surrendering it to you. I give you the behaviors, the teaching, the direction, and everything physical and spiritual in this room. Let your Spirit govern and rule in here today. Open my ears to your leading and fill my heart with the trust that you are here with us. Give me the face of Jesus today and bless us so all that happens today will be for our good and your glory.

Romans 8:9 (ESV)
You, however, are not in the flesh but in the Spirit, if in fact the Spirit of God dwells in you. Anyone who does not have the Spirit of Christ does not belong to him.

Isaiah 55:8-9 (ESV)
For my thoughts are not your thoughts, neither are your ways my ways, declares the LORD.
9 For as the heavens are higher than the earth, so are my ways higher than your ways and my thoughts than your thoughts.

Psalm 36:7-9 (ESV)
How precious is your steadfast love, O God! The children of mankind take refuge in the shadow of your wings. 8 They feast on the abundance of your house, and you give them drink from the river of your delights. 9 For with you is the fountain of life; in your light do we see light.

Surround Me

Surround me today with people and circumstances that will further your kingdom. Let your Spirit be known to everyone near me. Use me to share your Word and your love, that you will be glorified. I seek to be your vessel today; mold me to your purpose.

James 1:19-20 (ESV)
Know this, my beloved brothers: let every person be quick to hear, slow to speak, slow to anger; 20 for the anger of man does not produce the righteousness of God.

Isaiah 64:8 (ESV)
But now, O LORD, you are our Father; we are the clay, and you are our potter; we are all the work of your hand.

Psalm 16:9 (ESV)
Therefore my heart is glad, and my whole being rejoices; my flesh also dwells secure.

Tenderness

Help me to speak to my students with your tenderness. I want them to feel loved but sometimes I get caught up in the pace of the day and my answers are short and hurtful. Give me your peace and calm so I can reflect that to my students. It is your face I want them to see.

Proverbs 12:25 (ESV)
Anxiety in a man's heart weighs him down, but a good word makes him glad.

Philippians 4:8 (ESV)
Finally, brothers, whatever is true, whatever is honorable, whatever is just, whatever is pure, whatever is lovely, whatever is commendable, if there is any excellence, if there is anything worthy of praise, think about these things.

Psalm 25:4-5 (ESV)
Make me to know your ways, O LORD; teach me your paths. 5 Lead me in your truth and teach me, for you are the God of my salvation; for you I wait all the day long.

Thankful

Lord, I'm thankful for fellow teachers, staff, and administrators who follow you and who have a sense of cooperation and discernment. Let truth and fairness prevail in this building as we acknowledge you as Jehovah Jireh, the Provider. I pray that all I do today is for my good and your glory.

2 Chronicles 16:9 (ESV)
For the eyes of the LORD run to and fro throughout the whole earth, to give strong support to those whose heart is blameless toward him.

1 Chronicles 16:8 (ESV)
Oh give thanks to the LORD; call upon his name; make known his deeds among the peoples!

Psalm 7:17 (ESV)
I will give to the LORD the thanks due to his righteousness, and I will sing praise to the name of the LORD, the Most High.

Thanks for the Job

Your provisions and blessings are endless. Thank you for this job. I get up every morning knowing I have a calling and a purpose and you will be with me each passing hour. You carry me when I'm tired and push me when I need a boost. You put children in my classroom whose needs are greater than my ability to meet but you help them all endure. Thank you for this building and everything in it. Help me do everything I do today for your glory.

Romans 11:33-36 (ESV)
Oh, the depth of the riches and wisdom and knowledge of God! How unsearchable are his judgments and how inscrutable his ways! ³⁴ "For who has known the mind of the Lord, or who has been his counselor?" ³⁵ "Or who has given a gift to him that he might be repaid?"
³⁶ For from him and through him and to him are all things. To him be glory forever. Amen.

Luke 6:37-38 (ESV)
"Judge not, and you will not be judged; condemn not, and you will not be condemned; forgive, and you will be forgiven; ³⁸ give, and it will be given to you. Good measure, pressed down, shaken together, running over, will be put into your lap. For with the measure you use it will be measured back to you."

Psalm 57:1 (ESV)
Be merciful to me, O God, be merciful to me, for in you my soul takes refuge; in the shadow of your wings I will take refuge, till the storms of destruction pass by.

Thanksgiving

Thank you for these students and their families. You've placed each one in my room for a reason and I need your strength to meet the unending needs I'll see today. Open my eyes and reveal to me your path.

2 Samuel 22:47 (ESV)
"The LORD lives, and blessed be my rock, and exalted be my God, the rock of my salvation,

Proverbs 15:4 (NKJV)
A wholesome tongue is a tree of life, But perverseness in it breaks the spirit.

Psalm 119:125 (ESV)
I am your servant; give me understanding, that I may know your testimonies!

They Need You

I know that every student who enters here doesn't know you. Help me target the ones who will be lost; those that need your touch. Draw them to you and let me be the face of Jesus that they might learn to seek you above all else.

1 Chronicles 16:10-11 (ESV)
Glory in his holy name; let the hearts of those who seek the LORD rejoice! 11 Seek the LORD and his strength; seek his presence continually!

2 Corinthians 3:5 (ESV)
Not that we are sufficient in ourselves to claim anything as coming from us, but our sufficiency is from God,

Psalm 62:8 (ESV)
Trust in him at all times, O people; pour out your heart before him; God is a refuge for us. Selah

Time

Lord, I feel rushed as I run through each day; the hours flying by like minutes. Sometimes I do things automatically without thought or care. Sometimes I neglect things altogether because I don't take the time or act with great purpose. When you are the One I neglect, forgive me. Show me where I can make better use of my time to include the most important behavior of all; that of acknowledging you as my Lord and Savior. I will be blessed by spending time with you.

John 10:11 (ESV)
I am the good shepherd. The good shepherd lays down his life for the sheep.

James 1:17 (ESV)
Every good gift and every perfect gift is from above, coming down from the Father of lights with whom there is no variation or shadow due to change.

Psalm 34:19 (ESV)
Many are the afflictions of the righteous, but the LORD delivers him out of them all.

Tired

Lord, I'm tired. I find myself longing for rest, for quiet, for fewer things on my plate, for fewer responsibilities. This is a high-paced, intense and demanding job. I feel like I'm running all day. Renew me. Let your Spirit carry me when I can't take one more step and fill me with your hope and the promise of your peace. Help me hold on to all your promises to stay with me.

Matthew 11:28 (ESV)
Come to me, all who labor and are heavy laden, and I will give you rest.

1 Peter 5:6-7 (ESV)
Humble yourselves, therefore, under the mighty hand of God so that at the proper time he may exalt you, 7 casting all your anxieties on him, because he cares for you.

Psalm 27:14 (ESV)
Wait for the LORD; be strong, and let your heart take courage; wait for the LORD!

Trust

Often, I fall into a pattern of independence and I think I have to do everything and the weight of that weakens me. Help me trust that all your promises are true. You are always with me, you will never leave me, you are my strength and you are in control. Lord, I believe in your love for me and your desire to give me what I need in every circumstance. Keep my eyes and heart on these words from you during the busyness of my day.

Philippians 2:12-16 (ESV)
Therefore, my beloved, as you have always obeyed, so now, not only as in my presence but much more in my absence, work out your own salvation with fear and trembling, [13] for it is God who works in you, both to will and to work for his good pleasure. [14] Do all things without grumbling or disputing, [15] that you may be blameless and innocent, children of God without blemish in the midst of a crooked and twisted generation, among whom you shine as lights in the world, [16] holding fast to the word of life, so that in the day of Christ I may be proud that I did not run in vain or labor in vain.

Revelation 1:8 (ESV)
"I am the Alpha and the Omega," says the Lord God, "who is and who was and who is to come, the Almighty."

Psalm 27:4 (ESV)
One thing have I asked of the LORD, that will I seek after: that I may dwell in the house of the LORD all the days of my life, to gaze upon the beauty of the LORD and to inquire in his temple.

Vision

I become short sighted and consumed in students, problems, and daily demands. Sometimes I lose sight of your overall plan for me in my daily work. Help me slow down so I can better see what you see for me today, that I have clarity and see purpose for my students and me. Be my vision and broaden my view that I may see You, and others may see You in me.

1 Timothy 1:17 (ESV)
To the King of the ages, immortal, invisible, the only God, be honor and glory forever and ever. Amen.

Isaiah 55:6-7 (ESV)
"Seek the LORD while he may be found; call upon him while he is near; 7 let the wicked forsake his way, and the unrighteous man his thoughts; let him return to the LORD, that he may have compassion on him, and to our God, for he will abundantly pardon.

Psalm 119:27 (ESV)
Make me understand the way of your precepts, and I will meditate on your wondrous works.

Who Can I Help?

Show me who I can help today. Put someone in my path that needs an extra measure of encouragement or peace which can only be shared because of you. Fill me with what I need to extend that love that transforms us that someone else can be filled. Give me the words I need and the wisdom to recognize the opportunity you will provide.

1 Peter 1:8-9 (NRSV)

Although you have not seen him, you love him; and even though you do not see him now, you believe in him and rejoice with an indescribable and glorious joy, 9 for you are receiving the outcome of your faith, the salvation of your souls.

John 13:14 (ESV)

If I then, your Lord and Teacher, have washed your feet, you also ought to wash one another's feet.

Psalm 23:1-4 (ESV)

The LORD is my shepherd; I shall not want. 2 He makes me lie down in green pastures. He leads me beside still waters. 3 He restores my soul. He leads me in paths of righteousness for his name's sake. 4 Even though I walk through the valley of the shadow of death, I will fear no evil, for you are with me; your rod and your staff, they comfort me.

Wisdom

I do not claim to own my time today. You control my minutes and my hours. You know who needs me today and how they need me. Lead me to the student or the family where I can serve. Make them known to me and tell me what they need to hear or how I can be Jesus today.

James 4:8 (ESV)
Draw near to God, and he will draw near to you. Cleanse your hands, you sinners, and purify your hearts, you double-minded.

Titus 2:11-14 (ESV)
For the grace of God has appeared, bringing salvation for all people, 12 training us to renounce ungodliness and worldly passions, and to live self-controlled, upright, and godly lives in the present age, 13 waiting for our blessed hope, the appearing of the glory of our great God and Savior Jesus Christ, 14 who gave himself for us to redeem us from all lawlessness and to purify for himself a people for his own possession who are zealous for good works.

Psalm 13:5-6 (ESV)
But I have trusted in your steadfast love; my heart shall rejoice in your salvation. 6 I will sing to the LORD, because he has dealt bountifully with me.

Working for You

I pray for my job today. I am accountable to the district, the administration, my principal, and parents. I seek to fulfill my duties honestly. But I know I really answer to you, Lord, and I pray my day will reflect your love, wisdom and discernment in all my actions and words.

Hebrews 12:15 (ESV)
See to it that no one fails to obtain the grace of God; that no "root of bitterness" springs up and causes trouble, and by it many become defiled;

1 Thessalonians 5:16-18 (ESV)
Rejoice always, 17 pray without ceasing, 18 give thanks in all circumstances; for this is the will of God in Christ Jesus for you.

Psalm 27:1 (ESV)
The LORD is my light and my salvation; whom shall I fear? The LORD is the stronghold of my life; of whom shall I be afraid?

Worry

I confess that I worry. Problems at work seem overwhelming and I find myself worrying about them and allowing them to crowd into my thinking. In my heart, I know that you are in control and no amount of worrying will change the circumstances. Guide my thoughts so I rely on your wisdom and will, as you release the worry from me and take that burden. I submit to your will and ask for forgiveness for not trusting you enough. Thank you for taking the worry from me.

Romans 5:3-5 (ESV)
Not only that, but we rejoice in our sufferings, knowing that suffering produces endurance, [4] and endurance produces character, and character produces hope, [5] and hope does not put us to shame, because God's love has been poured into our hearts through the Holy Spirit who has been given to us.

Deuteronomy 33:27 (ESV)
The eternal God is your dwelling place, and underneath are the everlasting arms. And he thrust out the enemy before you and said, 'Destroy.'

Psalm 145:18-20 (ESV)
The LORD is near to all who call on him, to all who call on him in truth. [19] He fulfills the desire of those who fear him; he also hears their cry and saves them. [20] The LORD preserves all who love him, but all the wicked he will destroy.

You Are Sovereign

You alone stand above all others. No one is like you. You are perfect in all your ways; your wisdom, your love, your power. I acknowledge you as ruler of my heart and my life. It is you that I praise and serve today. Thank you for your sovereignty and for being a perfect and forgiving Father and Almighty King.

Exodus 15:13 (ESV)
"You have led in your steadfast love the people whom you have redeemed; you have guided them by your strength to your holy abode.

Ephesians 2:8-9 (ESV)
For by grace you have been saved through faith. And this is not your own doing; it is the gift of God, [9] not a result of works, so that no one may boast.

Psalm 57:9-10 (ESV)
I will give thanks to you, O Lord, among the peoples; I will sing praises to you among the nations. [10] For your steadfast love is great to the heavens, your faithfulness to the clouds.

Your Presence

Lord, fill our rooms, halls and offices with your presence today. Let your Spirit be evidenced by calm and quiet behavior, kindness, goodness, patience, and love. Let everyone who comes into this building feel the warmth that only comes from the power of the Holy Spirit and let them take that warmth and spread it into their homes and our community. Let this school be an agent of your love, Lord, and a place where your blessings abound.

Colossians 2:6-7 (ESV)
Therefore, as you received Christ Jesus the Lord, so walk in him, 7 rooted and built up in him and established in the faith, just as you were taught, abounding in thanksgiving.

Ephesians 5:8-10 (ESV)
for at one time you were darkness, but now you are light in the Lord. Walk as children of light 9 (for the fruit of light is found in all that is good and right and true), 10 and try to discern what is pleasing to the Lord.

Psalm 119:103-105 (ESV)
How sweet are your words to my taste, sweeter than honey to my mouth! 104 Through your precepts I get understanding; therefore I hate every false way. 105 Your word is a lamp to my feet and a light to my path.

Section Two:
Prayer
of the Day

Monday

Lord, it's the first day of our school week. Some of my students may have had a weekend full of fear or violence. Some may be tired from lack of refreshing sleep. Whatever the weekend has brought them, I pray that this room, this school, will be a haven of safety where the staff and teachers will show love and compassion to everyone. I surrender this room and everyone who enters, to you; trusting you for protection, love, and favor.

1 Peter 1:6-7 (NKJV)
In this you greatly rejoice, though now for a little while, if need be, you have been grieved by various trials, 7 that the genuineness of your faith, *being much more precious than gold that perishes, though it is tested by fire, may be found to praise, honor, and glory at the revelation of Jesus Christ,*

Proverbs 19:21 (NRSV)
The human mind may devise many plans, but it is the purpose of the LORD that will be established.

Psalm 143:8 (NKJV)
Cause me to hear Your lovingkindness in the morning, For in You do I trust; Cause me to know the way in which I should walk, For I lift up my soul to You.

Tuesday

Continue to fill this classroom with your loving presence. Move about in our hearts and fill us. Keep us mindful of the needs of others and how we can serve you by meeting these needs. Let kindness prevail and your will be done.

Hebrews 11:1 (ESV)
Now faith is the assurance of things hoped for, the conviction of things not seen.

Ephesians 2:4-5 (ESV)
But God, being rich in mercy, because of the great love with which he loved us, ⁵ even when we were dead in our trespasses, made us alive together with Christ—by grace you have been saved—

Psalm 144:15 (NRSV)
Happy are the people to whom such blessings fall; happy are the people whose God is the LORD.

Wednesday

We look to you today to provide all that we need. You will be our strength, our joy, and our comfort. We declare our dependence on you to steer us away from conflict and bind us together with your love. Give me a teacher's intuition and insight when trouble occurs and bless our learning time today.

Job 19:25 (ESV)
For I know that my Redeemer lives, and at the last he will stand upon the earth.

Luke 10:27 (ESV)
And he answered, "You shall love the Lord your God with all your heart and with all your soul and with all your strength and with all your mind, and your neighbor as yourself."

Psalm 51:10-12 (ESV)
Create in me a clean heart, O God, and renew a right spirit within me. 11 Cast me not away from your presence, and take not your Holy Spirit from me. 12 Restore to me the joy of your salvation, and uphold me with a willing spirit.

Thursday

Lord, help us make good progress in our learning today. Make things clear to students and allow me to focus on good teaching. Extend your love to my students through me so they know I love them. Ignite a respect and caring between classmates and teachers. Keep your banner of love over our building today.

1 Peter 1:14-16 (ESV)
As obedient children, do not be conformed to the passions of your former ignorance, 15 but as he who called you is holy, you also be holy in all your conduct, 16 since it is written, "You shall be holy, for I am holy."

Ephesians 2:10 (NRSV)
For we are what he has made us, created in Christ Jesus for good works, which God prepared beforehand to be our way of life.

Psalm 8:1-2 (ESV)
O LORD, our Lord, how majestic is your name in all the earth! You have set your glory above the heavens. 2 Out of the mouth of babies and infants, you have established strength because of your foes, to still the enemy and the avenger.

Friday

It's the end of our school week, Lord. You have blessed us each day and led us safely to the last day of our week. Comfort those who will experience struggles this weekend and let them feel your presence when they are alone. Keep all my students in good health and heal those that are sick. Protect them on their way home and let peace reign in their homes this weekend. Bless their families and let them be a positive encouragement in all circumstances. Keep your hand on them until you return them to me next week.

John 8:12 (ESV)
Again Jesus spoke to them, saying, "I am the light of the world. Whoever follows me will not walk in darkness, but will have the light of life."

Isaiah 40:29 (ESV)
He gives power to the faint, and to him who has no might he increases strength.

Psalm 18:35 (ESV)
You have given me the shield of your salvation, and your right hand supported me, and your gentleness made me great.

Section Three: Read, Recite, Repeat

Read, recite, and repeat Scripture all day:

My grace is sufficient for you.
2 Corinthians 12:9

The joy of the Lord is your strength.
Nehemiah 8:10

God is the strength of my heart and
my portion forever.
Psalm 73:26

He is for me! How can I be afraid?
Psalm 118:6

...do not fear, for I am with you...
Isaiah 41:10

I can do everything through him who
gives me strength.
Philippians 4:13

Come near to God and he will come near to you.
James 4:8

Cast all your anxiety on him because
he cares for you.
1 Peter 5:7

Nothing will be impossible for you.
Matthew 17:20

He giveth quietness.
Job 34:29

Trust in the Lord and do good; dwell in the land
and enjoy safe pasture.
Psalm 37:3

Pick your mantra and repeat as needed:

1. Jesus
2. See me
3. Thank you, Lord
4. I need you now, Lord
5. Here I am, Lord
6. I know you're with me
7. Give me strength (This was a favorite of my fifth-grade teacher...like all the time!)
8. I love you, Lord

Record your own and share with fellow teachers. I'm sure they could use them too.
_____
_____
_____
_____
_____
_____
_____

Section Four:
Devotions

It's All New

Greetings to all teacher friends and others! I took the summer off from writing and from everything really, and loved every minute of it. But all of a sudden, it's almost September and while I am not setting up a classroom, fall does bring a bit of "new." I know the trees shed old leaves, the grass needs no more attention, I will get rid of annuals in my pots, but for us Christians, there is newness. The newness comes in more than new school clothes, new shoes, new pencils, or even new classroom assignments. Our "new" comes in a "new heart and new spirit," (Ez. 18:31), in a "new life," (Rom. 6:4), "new birth into a living hope," (1 Peter 1:3), and God's compassions which are "new every morning," (Lam. 3:23.) The good news is that we can claim all this "new" every day of our lives, not just when a season changes or a new semester begins. Blessings to all of you as you start your "new" school year. Remember whose child you are and be blessed by the Lord and highly favored.

> "Sometimes when we get overwhelmed, we forget how big God is."

September Already?

No, it's only August. But we all know what August means. It's a mere prefix to September. And September brings with it different things to different people. To educators and anyone affiliated with a school, it means gearing up for another class or the responsibilities of running an office, and kids, and parents...and the list goes on. Our "free time" or that so-called 3-month vacation we all get as teachers, is about to come to a halt. (Don't you wish it really was 3 months long?)

The good news is the Lord didn't take a vacation nor does He need to gear up for your new semester. He's ready to lift you, guide you, and when needed (and needed He will be) He will sustain you. His power is perfect, his love unconditional, and his mercies are endless. Use his strength as you gear up and turn your thoughts towards September. Allow his truths to guide your thoughts and keep your focus on Him. Your burden will be too heavy no matter how excited and motivated you are. Give it to the Lord. He knows your tomorrow and He's ready for you.

I hope these words and words to follow will help you keep your direction clear and your burdens light. 1Chronicles 16:11 says, "Look to the Lord and his strength. Seek his face always." Tuck these words away and visit them September 4th. It can't hurt! Be blessed by the Lord and highly favored.

Overwhelmed?

Isaiah 43:2 says, "When you pass through the waters, I will be with you; and when you pass through the rivers, they will not sweep over you. When you walk through the fire, you will not be burned;" We heard this in church this morning as the pastor was addressing the topic of being OVERWHELMED, and what we can do when this happens.

My guess is there are several of you who are already feeling overwhelmed and you've completed only a few days of school. The advice we heard was the path Mary, the mother of our Lord, took when the angel told her she was going to have a baby. (Her feelings might be similar to what you might be feeling now, specifically in your job. Not to say there are no other areas that are overwhelming in your life.) What I heard was this: let go of the need to control the situation...we live in a broken world and don't always know ahead the path we walk because we walk by faith; let others help you out...we as teachers rely on each other all the time, and let God give you strength...we know we don't have enough for the job anyway so why not ask He Who is Most Powerful to be your strength?

My prayer for you this week is that while you acknowledge those times when you feel you are overwhelmed, you seek the face of Jesus, knowing He is ultimately in control and it is in Him you will find your rest. And the reprieve from feeling "overwhelmed." Be blessed by the Lord and highly favored.

My New Heart

In Ezekiel 36:26-27 God promised to restore Israel not only physically, but spiritually. It says, "I will give you a new heart and put a new spirit in you; I will remove from you your heart of stone and give you a heart of flesh. And I will put my Spirit in you and move you to follow my decrees and be careful to keep my laws." I believe this verse is meant for me too. Whether I am in a classroom, with my family, or enjoying the solitude of communing with my Lord, I have his Spirit living in me. It is that Spirit that shows love to students, family, or strangers. I can't do it alone but need the grace of my heavenly Father to work in me. Use this power or gift of grace to guide you today; to follow where you're led and love like only God can love. He's just doing it through you. Be blessed by the Lord and highly favored.

By Invitation

If you are a seasoned teacher, the past week may have seemed like very familiar repetition. You unpacked, arranged, and set up a room that would be welcoming to your students. If you are a new teacher, you did all that plus you were probably filled with a mixture of excitement and fear! Either way, I would invite you to do one more thing for your room. Invite the Holy Spirit to be a part of your preparation and eventually your life in that room. Invite Him to surround your students. Invite Him to hold you up. Invite Him to inspire you when you have no energy. Let Him guide your words and works and trust that you will feel His presence every day. I pray for God to reveal Himself to you from start to finish. Be blessed by the Lord and highly favored.

Sheep or Shepherd?

Let me preface my thoughts with this: When I say "teachers" I use the word to include anyone who interacts with children and is even remotely responsible for their education. No one in a school should be exempt. Having said that, let's think about our role in that educational process. In familiar Bible stories I grew up with, shepherds pop up many times and I thought how fun that might be; to walk along poking lambs and ewes, sitting quietly and watching them graze. On the other hand, the sheep, as it was pointed out to me later, are not the brightest of animals. They need a lot of guidance and prodding and are quite defenseless.

Jesus calls Himself the Good Shepherd. Like the shepherd in ancient times, lying down in the doorway of the fold to keep his flock safe, Jesus is also that door. It is through Him we must walk if we are to be kept safe and as humans, we too, are defenseless against evil if we are without a shepherd. So, what does that say to us as "teachers?" We sometimes are the sheep because our role finds us following someone else's guidance, rules, or prodding. Yet we have the awesome task of being the shepherd to our students. Our families expect that we will keep our students safe, guide them, provide for them and seek them out when they wander (wandering can happen in many ways).

As this week unfolds and many of us are returning to school to prepare our hearts, minds, and rooms for the beginning of another year, think of Jesus, your Shepherd, every time you walk through the doorway of your room, or your office, or even the front door. Whisper Jesus' name as you enter, asking Him to shepherd you and help you be the shepherd you need to be to your "sheep". Ask for His strength and guidance. It's there for you in abundance. Be blessed by the Lord and highly favored.

What's in a Name?

Quite possibly many of you learned some new names last week. The trick now is to remember them all. Your students have one name to remember but you...well you have many. Besides the Miss, Mrs., or Mr. you hear most often, do they sometimes call you "Teacher", or even "Mom", or I remember being called "Grandma" more than once. Early in my career I corrected many students every time they called me "Teacher", reminding them of my proper name. Then one day it occurred to me, I AM their teacher, and I love being their teacher, so who does it hurt if they call me that? Our Father God, Jesus, and the Holy Spirit have many names too. Think of as many as you can. (Father, Holy God, Redeemer, Savior, Rock, Refuge, Anchor, Comforter, and hundreds more.) I'm pretty sure we use different names to call on God depending on what's on our mind or what we're asking for. I'm thinking because our God is so many things to us, we see Him in many roles and He delights in hearing from us when we call upon Him. Your students see you in many loving ways too. Enjoy being their Teacher this week. Be blessed by the Lord and highly favored.

Hangin' On

It's the middle of September and I managed to get sunburned at the beach yesterday. The sun doesn't care what the season is. It still burns. While I was there I was reminded of the water show I watched a few weeks ago from the same spot. I sat fascinated while three men danced and sped all over the waves on small boards the size of skate boards. The difference was they were attached to long ropes that were then attached to sizable sails. Maybe sailboarding? I don't know the term but during this two-hour performance, I noticed how effortless they made it look. They held on, they followed the direction of the wind, they jumped and somersaulted in the air, landed on their feet, breezed into shore, turned and sped back out towards the deep, and started all over again. All the while they seemed carefree and safe. Never having seen this kind of "sport," I was mesmerized.

Then it came to me. These men were at the mercy of the wind and their sails. They probably were exerting a lot of energy but their level of expertise made it seem simple. It's like us. In life, we are at the mercy of a Holy God, connected to us by His Son, Jesus. God does all the controlling while we speed, jump, turn, expend energy, and try to act like we're in control. But if our wind shifts or dies down or we get in over our heads, we find we are really not in control at all. I want to remember every minute of every day and who really provides the ropes and the sails in my life. I'll hang on for safety, mercy, and goodness. Be blessed by the Lord and highly favored.

Keep Him Near

I trust you are feeling a little more comfortable with your fall schedule and you and your students are growing in a new and wonderful relationship. I know there are still some of you that are changing locations and classrooms. This can be a painful experience. I pray that if you are one of those who are moving, that you will find the blessings that will come in your new assignment.

Changing schools, grade levels, or even classrooms create an angst in us that is sometimes hard to reckon with. What do we do with those feelings? How do we keep our focus where it should be and off the very thing that demands all our energy? How about giving yourself a cue, something to redirect your attention; something that will remind you who you really are and what's important. My grandson was washing his hands in school one day and as he was drying them, he noticed that the soap he had used (I'm glad he even used soap!) reminded him of me. He told his mom that night that his hands smelled like Grandma so he found himself smelling his hands all day so he could feel close to me. It does create sort of a weird picture but I found it endearing.

Your challenge might be to find something to look at, hold, or yes, even smell, that will create in you a peace that will allow you to be the teacher you were created to be, changing that angst you were feeling into a calm confidence. We don't have to be a re-assigned teacher to look for that cue. We could all benefit from a constant reminder of someone who loves us and grants us His peace.

Easy Access

Where do you wish you could go? How often would you want to go? How easy would the trip be? What I'm thinking of right now is easy access to my neighbor's house. There is one common neighbor's backyard separating the two of us and in the summer, we can walk through grass and a few stray bushes and within a minute, we can be sitting together over iced tea and hilarious conversation. I love it. It's like an extension of my own yard and the years of friendship are evident to both of us. But in the winter, deep snow and lately, perilous ice, have prohibited easy access for both of us. I really miss that. I can still walk down the driveway, follow the sidewalk, and climb her driveway and there I am, but that easy access in the backyard has become the norm. Easy access may be something I will continue to seek the older I become. But think of the easy access we have to our Father-all year long. Deep snow, perilous ice, pelting rain, nothing matters. No backyards impair our access and with a repentant heart and faith in Jesus as our newborn Redeemer, God is accessible every minute of every day.

It couldn't be easier. Remember to "access" Him this busy season. He doesn't get too busy for us and longs for us as His children. Be blessed by the Lord and highly favored.

Seasons Change

It's hard not to think about the season changing right now; the colors are so vibrant, the temperature changes by the day, the sun is out then it's rainy, reports come in of snow, then the next day it's beautiful again. The raking has started, people are pulling in their porch furniture, rolling up their hoses and preparing to hunker down for the cold and winter.

Come spring, we'll see more changes. The leaves will come back, the outdoor furniture will return, the lawn mowers will replace the snow blowers, and you'll probably see your neighbors again! The changes we see serve as time markers for us; visible evidence of time passing. Many of the things I just mentioned are predictable and fairly painless. They're expected and even anticipated with a feeling of welcome. But what will we be doing in this next season? Will anything change with us? Will we grow into something else or move through something, or experience some painful change? The changes that we might encounter may not be so welcomed or anticipated with joy and are not really predictable at all.

We are at the mercy of our Creator. He knows the future, the minute by minute passing of every day. Everything that will happen to us or has happened to us has been ordained by Him.

No harm will come that He doesn't already know about and He's prepared to give us what we need to deal with that season.

So as you witness the changes in our visible world, watch for changes in your personal season. You might even be intentional about initiating a change that you've been wanting to make. In our busy jobs where we are constantly doing for others and meeting everyone else's expectations, consider thinking about making a spiritual change or a "next move" or an "upgrade." What do you think the Lord wishes you would change? Ask Him for help or guidance in making a seasonal change that will be for your good and His glory. Be blessed by the Lord and highly favored.

Hold the Rod

Do you know the story in the Bible about Joshua fighting Amalek? The only way Joshua could prevail over Amalek was when Moses was holding his rod above his head. When his arms got tired and the rod was lowered, Joshua would begin to lose. Aaron and Hur helped Moses hold his arms up under the weight of the rod until Joshua finally defeated Amalek.

This story made me think of life's battles today. We can't really fight them alone. We don't have the strength. If we're lucky we have friends or colleagues that will help us fight the battles; friends to pray with us and support us. As teachers, we all face common problems and battles and having a "team" to lean on is a blessing we don't want to be without. Go to your "Aaron and Hur" today and thank them for helping you hold up the rod. May you be blessed by the Lord and highly favored.

Hand Written

Have you ever had your handwriting analyzed? I haven't but I am aware that there are people that have studied this science and can tell a lot about you by the way you write. While looking through holiday recipes the other day, I ran across a card in my mother's handwriting. It hit me hard because of her recent passing. There will be no more recipes passed down in her handwriting. I have what I have.

Then it hit me. I am familiar with how she wrote her letters. I could identify her words if you scrambled them up with someone else's. Don't you wonder how that happens? There are 26 letters but everyone writes them down in their own peculiar way. I was thinking about how Scripture was written. These are the most important words we'll ever read and they, too, can be recognized and identified as belonging to a specific Author. What we do with these Words is up to us. I know I love to read letters hand written by a friend or family member. I read and reread them and they warm my heart. God wrote, hand wrote, letters, lessons, and stories for us and they are bound together for us to read and reread. These words should guide us and prompt us to share what's in them and follow the messages.

As we give thanks in this season, I'm thankful the Lord has chosen to write to me; to send me a letter personally and to love me through His Words. Be blessed by the Lord and highly favored.

A Bittersweet Good-Bye

The school year started and I felt rather removed from all of you and your first days. I was consumed with family matters as my elderly mother spent a week in the hospital and 4 days in a nursing home before going to be with Jesus last night. It was the sweetest of good-byes but still hard to do.

Isn't it amazing what happens when we really submit our wills to the Lord and watch Him work? Much of what happened with my mom these last 10-11 days, was totally out of my control and while it seemed the doctors and nurses were the caretakers, it was evident that even these strangers were being led by the Lord's hand. I was given peace at every turn and discernment with decisions. We never felt frustrated or fearful but trusted that everything was happening just how the Lord ordained it.

The lesson for all of us in this process might be to ask for wisdom when we need it, listen for the voice that delivers it, and accept the peace and comfort that follows. Because follow it will! God promises us that. I pray that your first days with your new students have been exciting and fun. You are the Jesus they need to see so ask for that guidance and strength as you need it. It's there in abundance. Be blessed by the Lord and highly favored.

Thankfulness

I only need to look at the calendar or listen to the radio to turn my thoughts to the approaching holiday. I always loved Thanksgiving. What's not to love with a fantastic meal and less stress than the hustle and bustle of Christmas? Everyone talks about all the things they are thankful for and we try to model for our kids the importance of being thankful for everything we have; our abundance, health, home, etc. The older I get, my thankfulness changes. Not that I'm not thankful for all the things mentioned here, but maybe it's age that changes perspective.

During a recent trip to my small hometown to bury my mother, I saw family I hadn't seen in forty years and special friends I've had for over fifty-five years! I realized how thankful I was to still have all of them; that each one is irreplaceable and filled my heart to overflowing. Imagine how much our Lord loves us. We love with a human heart and He IS love! He loves us so that we have love to pass around...whether to our family, students, or friends. He IS love so we HAVE love. I'm thankful His pure love depends on nothing I do but solely on His mercy and grace; his mercy, grace, and love. Now these are reasons to be grateful. Have a happy Thanksgiving; blessed by the Lord and highly favored.

Path of My Prayers

The path I cut with our snow blower takes nothing more than a pull of the starter and a little gas and oil. No pleading or communication needed. The conversation I have with my cousin after not speaking to her in person for months, requires no effort because our relationship consists of one long conversation with very long pauses. But what about the path of my prayers? For me, that takes a little effort and some words; very specific words that will clear the path and open a way for my words to make their way to God's ear. Clutter falls into my life and chokes out goodness and forgiveness leaving behind the litter that will stand in the way of the petitions and thanks I am trying to pray. For my prayers to be acceptable to God, even with my Precious Savior interceding, I need to clear out the clutter and debris that is in the way. That means I start my prayers with confession. I ask the Lord to reveal to me any unconfessed sin that is in me so I can confess it. I declare my forgiveness for others so I can be open to His forgiveness for me. That begins to open the path of my prayers so I can present my thanks, praise, and petitions and nothing will be standing in the way to stop my prayers. We are always in a season full of reasons to pray often and love much. Keep prayer paths open. We don't want to miss one thing the Lord has in store for us. Be blessed by the Lord and highly favored.

Time to Make Noise

I'm sure, as teachers, we have all had days when we say, "1-2-3-eyes on me," or we flash the lights, or we clap our hands or raise our hands (hoping students will see us) and the whole point of whatever we do is to get everyone to be quiet. If they would just listen! Then there are those times of the day when we allow the noise and in fact, hope that the noise and movement will transform students into better, quieter learners later.

Believe it or not, there are times for us, as adults, where we should not be silenced; where we are free to make some noise, and offer celebration. One of those times is now, at Easter. Now is when we should be shouting our loudest and lifting our hands the highest. I love the account in Luke 19 where Jesus is riding into Jerusalem on the donkey and people around him are yelling, "Blessed is the king who comes in the name of the Lord!" They are making so much noise, it is making the Pharisees nervous and they ask Jesus to keep his people quiet. Jesus' reply is, "I tell you...if they keep quiet, the stones will cry out." v. 40. It's as if this message of praise, Jesus' impending sacrificial death, His gift to us, this act that would save all who choose to believe, is so magnificent, so miraculous, that it cannot be squelched. It must come out! It cannot be held in.

This Easter weekend we celebrate the greatest gift of all. But we can make noise about it all year through. Share your joy with someone and make some noise about your Redeemer, Creator, and Risen Lord. Be blessed by the Lord and highly favored.

Prayer

If you're anything like me, prayer isn't new to you. What IS new to me is this idea: Prayer is not specific words said at a prescribed time in a certain way. Prayer is a relationship with the Lord. It is continuous and can be as easy and automatic as breathing. It is where we start every morning and end every night. It happens when we are thankful and when we are full of fear; hurting, discouraged, happy or sad. Our God wants to hear from us when everything is going well or when we're overwhelmed. He will listen to our anger and loves to hear our praises. All He wants is to deepen the relationship we have with Him and when we pray, we are communicating with the One who is sovereign and in control. Whatever our circumstances are, good, bad, or ugly, God is still good. He doesn't change just because we do. He is constant, faithful, and all His promises are true. So, try lifting every "thing" to the Lord today and give Him the burdens, thank Him for His blessings, and praise Him for who He is. Be blessed by the Lord and highly favored.

Oooo- Oooo Pick Me!

I remember asking questions in my classroom. Teachers ask a lot of questions. And then what do you do? I used to look around and decide just who I was going to call on for the answer. Do I call on the one who always gets it right? Do I call on someone ignoring me, hoping to "jar" them into paying attention? Do I call on someone who probably won't get it right but if they did it would boost their confidence? What's my purpose here? I would scan the crowd of desks and in a nanosecond, I would weigh all the options and call out a name. My heart would rejoice at a correct answer or I'd feel a bit unsuccessful if someone got stumped. I would much rather hear the right answer and think I had taught them something! Compare that with God. It says in 2 Chronicles 16:9, "The eyes of the Lord range throughout the earth to strengthen those whose hearts are fully committed to Him." He looks around to see who is ready; who needs what God has to give to finish His work on earth. Who is willing? Who knows the desires of God's heart and needs His strength to complete the work? Personally, I want to be the one with my hand waving in the air like our students do when they're bursting with eagerness to get the teacher's attention. I want the Lord to see me and count on me to do His work. Isn't that our job? Isn't that why we're here? To glorify Him? To develop that relationship with Him so that we know His desires and how to serve Him? Pick me, Teacher! Pick me, Lord! Be blessed by the Lord and highly favored.

Now I lay me down to sleep
I pray the lord my toys to keep
If I die before I wake
I pray the lord my toys to break
So no other kid can use them
Amen

By - Shel Silverstein

Strength for the Asking

I have a pillow that is embroidered with Scripture. It says, "I can do all things through Christ who strengthens me. Philippians 4:13." I have read it a thousand times, I've heard it in sermons, and I've heard people in conversations say that they rely on Christ's strength when they have none. But how does that work? How do we actually get strength from Christ? I believe the answer lies in a promise Jesus made two thousand years ago. He knew He would be leaving this earth but promised a Holy Spirit would take his place. We are promised that when we accept Jesus as our Savior the Holy Spirit takes up residence inside us. That's what gives us the "strength for the asking" when we think we have none. The same power that raised Christ from the dead is available to us...through that same Spirit that indwells every believer. So, every morning when you think you can't face whatever trial is ahead of you, seek the face of Jesus, God's loving arms, and the power of the Holy Spirit. God is in control of your day and He has way more resources than you do! Be blessed by the Lord and highly favored.

Free Courtesy Ticket

Last week I went shopping in Hastings. I had never been there despite its proximity to Grand Rapids. Driving through town for the first time, everyone in the car was taken with its charm and quaint appearance. We shopped a little, found a nice place to eat, shopped a little more, and just enjoyed having fun on a beautiful, cool, crisp fall day. Then we headed back to the car. I sat down behind the wheel and noticed a little yellow envelope tucked under my windshield wiper. You know the feeling you get in your stomach when you see flashing lights pulling up behind you or...you see the dreaded notice on your windshield. I grabbed it and read, "City of Hastings Police Department Parking Violation Ticket." I checked the sign on the curb thinking I had been quite careful where I parked and noticed a two-hour limit posted. My heart sank. Then I read further. Everywhere there was a dollar sign to show amount owed, I saw, $0.00. Despite the fine chart on the back of this notice, I had no fine. I breathed a sigh of relief, thought about the leniency granted to me, and thanked the Lord for the gift. As I was thanking Him, I thought, "Wow. That's a lot like how I can feel every day when I feel the Lord's mercy and grace for all the 'illegal' things I commit in my sinful life." I felt extreme gratitude to the police in Hastings for the forgiven debt shown to me in my "Free Courtesy Ticket." How much more am I indebted to my Creator for the ever-present mercy He shows all the time! Be blessed by the Lord and highly favored. Receive His mercy and pass it on.

Meditate on This

I'm taking a class called, "Solitude, Meditation, and Prayer." Our pastor is an awesome teacher and I respect his interpretation and appreciate his delivery. We are encouraged to meditate on several verses of Scripture each week, finding some time of solitude to do this. This week I chose Psalm 119:10-16. Several years ago, I chose these same passages as memory work and while it sounds very familiar and I can fill in many phrases, I can't say as I totally memorized it. Our goal in meditating is not memorizing but I find myself in my daily walk, wishing I could pull some of God's Words out of my head and actually use them; for myself or for others. So, this week my meditation has been dual purposed. What I found was the same premise I used in my classroom. Repetition-Repetition-Repetition. As I read and reread and reread and tried to connect the words so I could remember them, I began to develop so much more meaning to the verses. Here they are. I hope they bless you today. "I seek you with all my heart; do not let me stray from your commands. I have hidden your word in my heart that I may not sin against you. Praise be to you, O Lord; teach me your decrees. With my lips, I recount all the laws that come from your mouth. I rejoice in following your statutes as one rejoices in great riches. I meditate on your precepts and consider your ways. I delight in your decrees; I will not neglect your Word." Be blessed by the Lord and highly favored.

Keys of the Kingdom

I wish to share with you an idea I got from God's Best for My Life, by John Ogilvie. He based his idea on Matthew 16:19. It says, "And I will give you the keys of the kingdom of heaven, and whatever you bind on earth will be bound in heaven, and whatever you loose on earth will be loosed in heaven." Ogilvie goes on to say that Jesus has given US the keys of the kingdom and we use these keys to unlock the various kinds of doors we meet in other people. There is a key of listening, a key of discussion, a key of witness, prayer for another, and the key of unchanging love. We can use these keys to admit people to the kingdom or we can block them if we don't share what we know or have found.

My favorite sentence says, "We have the power to forgive in His name and to assure people of His love." What an awesome responsibility! What will you do this week with the keys that have been given to you? Be blessed by the Lord and highly favored.

Focus

What is your focus? And if I knew the plural of "focus," I could ask you about many of your "foci"? As teachers and staff in school buildings, we probably feel inundated with stimuli all day long and what we thought was going to be a focus, becomes just one little part of our day; maybe not even a very important one. How does this happen? I remember the speed at which I had to think on my feet and change direction by the minute sometimes. Kids demanding attention, my lesson demanding some attention, hopefully, and then there's those that I answered to as a staff member and employee. The list goes on. And it could be different every day. But what does the Lord say about my focus? Do you think He doesn't care about our daily responsibilities and distractions? He tells us plainly in Philippians 4:8, "Finally, brothers, whatever is true, whatever is noble, whatever is right, whatever is pure, whatever is lovely, whatever is admirable-if anything is excellent or praiseworthy-think about such things."

So where do you see things in your day that are true, noble, right, pure, lovely, admirable, excellent or praiseworthy? On any given day, you most certainly can and do witness these kinds of things, but on other days, doesn't it seem impossible to find? I don't have an answer as to how you keep your focus on the above command. But I do think that by knowing that that's where the Lord wants our thoughts and by watching for them or modeling them, we will increase our chances of experiencing the kind of focus that's good for our hearts and glorifying to God. Be blessed by the Lord and highly favored.

Kindness is a Secret

Where does kindness come from? If you had to explain it to someone just learning the English language, what would you say? You can't hold it; you can just see evidence of it like when we "see" the wind. You can't smell it or taste it, but maybe you can feel it. You might use words like, "helping others, doing something nice, or encouraging someone." But really, kindness looks different to different people.

Last year, I was reading some student work on a wall at one of the schools I visit. I don't remember if there was a picture or just the writing but it said, "Kindness is the best secret language." I wrote it down in my collection of things to write about someday thinking it was worth some thought, not really knowing what the student was thinking when they wrote it or if it was even original. But wherever it came from, I think it tells us kindness is another language we can use to communicate with just like our learned oral language. Maybe the secrecy comes into play because it's not taught by textbooks.

It's observed or modeled and it can be learned or ignored. There are countless references to "kind" or "kindness" in the Bible. "A kind word cheers you up." Proverbs 12:25, "Blessed is he who is kind to the needy," Proverbs 14:21, "kind to the oppressed," Deuteronomy 4:27, "He is kind to the ungrateful," Luke 6:35, "Love is kind," 1 Corinthians 13:4, "Be kind and compassionate," Ephesians 4:32 and on and on. We read these verses and because we read them in God-breathed Scripture, we know they're true. It really isn't much of a secret at all. It's more of a command. It's what Jesus was all about and it's our goal to make modeling this "best secret language" not so secret any more. Be blessed by the Lord and highly favored.

Who's in the Tree?

I would like to say every devotion I write comes right out of my own experience or my heart. But sometimes I read something and I feel compelled to share it. I find a nugget in someone else's writing and off I go. This is the case today. The idea came from a small devotional by Charles Stanley from June of last year. What he wrote was not intended for teachers but it is certainly applicable.

Who hasn't been discouraged by a student or maybe a parent? In our district, probably discouragement comes daily. We serve some underprivileged, some under achievers, high poverty, low motivation, broken-in-many-ways families. Depending on where you teach, you may see that daily. But I don't mean to make it sound like there's no hope. You really can't make a successful career in an environment where you don't see hope.

What I'm saying is that you ARE the hope. You are the servant here. You are the constant in someone's chaos; the light in a very dark world for some of them. Just as Jesus spent time with the outcasts, the sinners, the sick, the rejected, you too, have a calling. Stanley (2012) likened Jesus' visit with Zacchaeus to an opportunity to serve a "spiritually needy" man. He looked up a tree and intentionally singled him out by saying He would join him at his house; Zacchaeus, a despised tax collector in need of a Savior.

Jesus took the time to look up and pursue a relationship with someone in need. Not unlike what you do every day in your job. No doubt you will find someone up a tree today, waiting and hoping for a teacher, a secretary, or a principal to be available, aware, and accepting just like Jesus. Who's in your tree today? We'll pray that you will have what it takes to look up and be willing to serve. You are, after all, blessed by the Lord and highly favored.

Passion

I remember thinking many times in my classrooms, "They just aren't excited about learning. They have no passion to understand! If I could just engage them and set them on fire about learning! They don't seem teachable." I'm sure my lessons were somewhat adequate and interested some students, but there were always those that I didn't seem to reach. I found it hard to create curiosity; to create a passion for learning. I'm pretty sure they had a passion for something...could have been video games but it surely wasn't school.

What about our lives? Do we feel passion for the right things? What does a passion for Christ do for us? Have you ever felt it? We could have an ever-increasing hunger to know Him more thereby showing His righteousness as we live our daily lives. We could recognize how He works through our suffering for our growth and our good. We could know all this or we could act like many of our students and feed our passions for something other than the most important relationship we could have. As believers, we can model a passion for Christ even in our classrooms and pray that it is contagious; that someone who watches us could want what we have. We could try feeding our students' passions as we grow in ours. Christ is our hope, He is in us, and so we can be hope for someone else. Be blessed by the Lord and highly favored.

Transformation

I read a devotional this morning written by one of my favorite writers, Sarah Young. She helped my understanding of what happens when we allow the Lord to transform our darkness into light. Given a choice, I would choose light as opposed to darkness. Most people probably would. But we live in a broken, dark world. Without the light that Jesus brings to us every day, the "dark" is all we would be able to see. We are asked to live in the world but not be of the world. A trick? Sometimes, but really, if we let Jesus be our Light, keep Him and his hope in us, allow Him to guide our steps and surrender to his will, it is his Light that will let us see, obey, trust, and live in the darkness of our world. He has promised us that. We are not promised a perfect world. But we are promised a Light to help us in our world. What else do we need? Allow yourself to be transformed. Allow Light on your path.

Check out Psalm 18:28: "You, O Lord, keep my lamp burning; my God turns my darkness into light." And Psalm 119:105: "Your word is a lamp to my feet and a light for my path." Take solace in these Words. They are God-breathed and written for you. Be blessed by the Lord and highly favored.

Changing a Stone

Have you ever felt ineffective? Like you can't make a difference no matter what you do or how you say it or how many times you try? Sometimes it feels like what I'm trying to do is comparable to  changing a stone. I love stones. They are in bowls, baskets, piles, plants, and buckets all over my house. I love the colors and patterns; the shapes. And I would never try or want to change any of them. But the other day I was having my quiet time with the Lord in my living room. In front of me on the coffee table sits a bowl of stones from Lake Superior. I picked up 3 of them to hold in my hand while I was praying. They were cold to the touch but I held them for enough time to transfer my body heat to them. I put them down when I was done then remembered someone I had forgotten to pray for so I picked them up again but of course, I didn't pay attention to which 3 I had originally chosen. As I grabbed them I noticed one of them was cold. I thought, "Wow, these 2 have been changed. They're different. I can even change a stone!"

I immediately thought how we're changed by God. He probably sees us as stones sometimes. His touch is what will change us. But just as the stones in my bowl will grow cold again without my touch, we need God's hand on us continually to keep us in His will, surrendered, and obedient. Staying connected to Him allows us to be the conduit between Him and our students, or family, or this broken world. We really can change stones. Teachers are living proof. With God's help, we do it every day.

Not Meant to Be Like This

I found this quote by Timothy Keller. It says: "Our Christian hope is that we're going to live with Christ in a new earth, where there is not only no more death, but where life is what it was always meant to be." It was an "a-ha" moment for me when I read it. Our lives are not what they were supposed to be. As teachers, we aren't supposed to have children from broken homes. Homes weren't intended to be broken. We aren't supposed to have children with multiple disorders and diagnoses where learning becomes an insurmountable challenge. Disorders weren't supposed to happen. Poverty, abuses, addictions...none of these household words were supposed to happen. They weren't part of God's original plan.

But we live with them. They are part of our lives and our classrooms are the showrooms of the society we're in; broken, poor, neglected, challenged, hungry, unloved, and the list goes on. These words only begin to describe what you might face at work. Your work is a mission field. It's the real world; a microcosm of a world created by a perfect God but occupied by sin. Don't let that sin get in your way or come between you and the children in your care. They are the product of a sinful world and you may be the only light they see all day. It's your job to embrace the reality of "what really wasn't supposed to be." Not supposed to be, but really is. We certainly can't overlook or dismiss all the challenges in our classrooms but I believe it is our responsibility to love unconditionally whoever comes to us. That's how Jesus lived and I think He wants us to do the same. Be blessed by the Lord and highly favored.

Be Still and Know that I Am God

As believers, we live much of our lives in "trust" mode. This isn't a bad place to be but sometimes it doesn't feel like solid ground. I have been spending a lot of time in this mode since the passing of my mother. I share this with you because part of the legacy that she left me makes for a great devotion.

 Her favorite verse in the Bible was that very familiar Psalm 46:10, "Be still and know that I am God." After her passing I wondered what that meant to her and then started wondering what it really meant to me. I did a little research in preparation for what I would share at her memorial service and found the second half of that verse. It says, "I will be exalted among the nations, I will be exalted in the earth." My notes explained the meaning further for me. They said, "Reverently honor him and his power and his majesty. Take time each day to be still and exalt God." I knew then and there that was what my mom wanted me to remember.

MacArthur (2005) explains in his commentary, "These twin commands to not panic and to recognize his sovereignty are probably directed to both his nation for comfort and all other nations for warning." This part grabbed me and made me pause. Telling the nations that did not accept God that they should be still and know that He is really God and a God that they should exalt, comes out as a warning! But what a comfort those same words are to us, His children. He is our Father and uses those words to tell us that. I marvel at how those same words are both warning and comfort.

> *Prayer is when you talk to God; meditation is when you listen to God.*
>
> – Diana Robinson –

I would encourage anyone to spend some time meditating on those very words. Being still isn't always an easy thing to do these days, but God deserves our highest praise and being still can reveal His welcome comfort. Be blessed by the Lord and highly favored.

From the Good Book

Maybe some of you grew up hearing the phrase "the Good Book" when someone was referring to the Bible. It never meant to me then, what it does now; like many things in life. Today I just want to send out a couple of my favorite verses from the Good Book. Read, reflect, and here's a good one, ruminate. (Rumination is something a cow does to its food; chewing it over and over. No more details necessary.) Let these words be your refuge today.

"My mind and my body may grow weak, but God is my strength; He is all I ever need."   Psalm 73:26

"The steps of the godly are directed by the Lord. He delights in every detail of their lives. Though they stumble, they will not fall, for the Lord holds them by the hand."   Psalm 37:23-24

This second verse creates a great visual in my mind. I see the Lord holding my hand as I plod or skip or am dragged through the day and no matter my gait, the Lord can keep me steady. That's a good thing as I am really no good to Him on my face!

Pick a part or phrase of any of these verses and use them as your mantra today. Let the Lord into the details of your life. He delights in them. Be blessed by the Lord and highly favored.

Ten Days is Too Long

When my grandson, Daniel, was about 5 years old, I took a trip to Thailand with some friends. Daniel and I were usually attached at the hip; breakfast and school routines, spent the day in the same school building, picked him up at daycare, ate supper together, bath, brush and bedtime, and prayers - a blessing for me.

We had never been apart for more than 1 or 2 nights since he was born. I knew I would miss him but being the traveler is easier than being the one left behind. Upon returning to the airport after being gone for 10 days, I remember seeing Daniel running towards me at the gate and leaping into my arms. He frantically grabbed my face, looked me square in the eyes and said, "Grandma, 10 days is too long!" I couldn't have said it better myself.

10 days was too long. Too long for us to be apart, too long before we could talk and cuddle and read; too long not to just plain be together. I wonder what the Lord thinks is too long. How long does He have to wait to see me read His word? How long before I turn to Him and pray? Give Him thanks? Ask for help? Praise Him?

Not just that but what kind of time goes by between the times I reach out to someone, say "I love you", show kindness to strangers, forgive someone who hurt me, apologize to my spouse, tell someone about Jesus, invite someone to church, volunteer where I'm needed, feed the hungry, show Christ's love? Days, weeks, longer? How long is too long? Do I have to do all those things all the time?

I believe the answer is yes. Yes, because we are Christ followers and created in the image of God. We were created to have a relationship with our Father and as His children, we are responsible to act on His behalf. That means in our homes with our families, at work with our bosses and peers, and on the streets in our community. Jesus didn't serve every 10 days or when He felt like it. He was obedient and fully surrendered to His Father's will. I believe it is our job to follow the Master. Ten days is too long. Be blessed by the Lord and highly favored.

A New Coffee Pot

We bought a new coffee pot. That may not seem worthy of thought regarding a devotion but I think I found relevance. The coffee pot came with an instruction booklet but this is not our first coffee pot. We know to wash the parts before using, where to put water and where to put filters. My husband can usually even set the clock and auto timer without the instructions. Morning number one I walked into the kitchen before the auto start kicked on. I simply turned the knob to "brew" and it started up. This model has an "auto off" feature where it will stay on "warm" for up to four hours then shut off. I wondered what else it could do that I hadn't investigated yet. I would guess that much of my life could be enhanced or at least made simpler if I took the time to "read before assembling," or "starting," or "washing," or "cooking."

My mind immediately went to the Bible. When I thought of the "Instruction Manual" for the coffee pot, I thought of the "Instruction Manual for My Life." I wouldn't expect my life with God to be enhanced or even maintain any measure of quality if I didn't spend time reading the manual that comes with Him. The Bible was written for my life; what I'm to follow, how I should live, how I should act, whom I should glorify. It teaches, it convicts, it demonstrates love, forgiveness and justice. By accepting it as absolute truth I get to spend an eternity with my creator. Some manuals may improve my life here on earth if I study and apply them but God's Manual is different. His Manual IS my life. Be blessed by the Lord and highly favored.

All in the Family

Have you ever heard your child come up with a question you never thought of and later thought to yourself, "Where did that come from?" That happened to me one day when my grandson, Daniel, and I were riding in the car. He was in his car seat in the back and his query began like this: "God is Jesus' Father, right?" I answered, "Yes, that's right." He continued, "And we love the Father, right?" "Yes, we do." Here comes his deduction: "Well, if we love the Father, we gotta love the Son!" Yes, I guess we do!

Daniel was about four years old when he shared this bit of wisdom with me and I have smiled as I have recalled it many times since then. It makes me think of how we love others. How does that happen? Why am I almost instantaneous friends with some people and others it takes time and effort and then sometimes nothing grows?

It is the connection I feel with other believers that strikes the parallel with Daniel's questions and comment about loving the Son if we love the Father; that family thing. That's what knowing other believers feels like; family; an instant connection. It is something familiar. And what better, more solid connection could there be than the love of our Father on all of His children? And our reciprocal love...to the Father and the Son, because if you love the Father, ya 'gotta love the Son. Be blessed by the Lord and highly favored.

A Weekend of Praise with Michael W. Smith

"Thirty-seven-year-old daughter survived heart attack, triple bypass surgery. God answered prayer that she would turn to Christ. Her 17-yr. old son met his mom at the altar to see her accept Christ. I deserve chance to praise God, proclaim His goodness. My daughter's new life, for His glory."

These are the words I submitted to a contest some years ago. A contest I was absolutely sure I was going to win. I was so sure I was the winner that after a breakfast out with a colleague from work, we sat in the car in the restaurant parking lot listening to the radio show where I was going to hear my name as the winner. I can't remember being so sure of anything in my life. I had honed and pruned and chosen every word so carefully capturing the essence of the intensity of why I should be the one to enjoy a trip to Michael W. Smith's house and spend a weekend praising God with him.

We sat in the front seats and I waited nervously listening for the radio to announce, "Barb Quist!" I could just imagine me packing my suitcase and flying off to Tennessee when suddenly, they said----well I don't know what they said. But it wasn't Barb Quist. I sat flabbergasted; stunned. At first I thought maybe they had made a mistake. Was this the right contest result we were tuned into? How could it be? They didn't pick me. But my words were compelling. They were convincing. The whole idea was beautiful and heart-warming and a testimony to God. Who could have sent in a better 50-word essay than that? Suddenly I realized this contest had become about ME. I wanted to be the winner. I wanted the prize. I should be rewarded. I had taken the focus off the content; off the reason I wrote to begin with. I missed the point.

God has only one focus: me, us, His children. I need to have one focus as well and with God already focusing on me, I don't need to. My focus needs to be on my Creator, my Savior, the Only Wise God, The King of the Universe. I'm already a winner. And Jesus is the only Prize I'll ever need (Although I really do enjoy Michael W. Smith's music!). Be blessed by the Lord and highly favored.

Already There

Casting Crowns has a song called, "Already There." I have sung it a hundred times but listened to the words carefully just recently. I was blessed by the meaning that was made clear to me.

In essence, the words tell me that my life, as I see it from my limited perspective, is chaotic; full of fears and questions. But Jesus is already at the end of my life waiting for me and ready to join me there so that I can look back at my life with Him and He can show me the grand design He had for me. The chaos will have come together in His picture-perfect plan. I will see how all the pieces fit and what is my future now will then be a memory.

These words caused me to think about what my life will look like when I stand with the Lord and look back. I think I will see valleys where I struggled but grew as the Lord refined me. And I will see I wasn't alone. I will see peaks of hope and joy and again, I wasn't alone. I will also see chasms where the earth seems to have fallen away and a bridge was built to help me across. That bridge is carved out of rock, My Rock, My Creator God. And again, I was not alone.

My thoughts on death, my death in particular, do not disturb me nor frighten me. I am grateful for each day the Lord gives me and pray that I bring Him glory in every one of them. At the same time, I look with joyful anticipation to the day I meet Jesus face to face and see those I love that are "already there." Be blessed by the Lord and highly favored.

Follow the (Your) Leader

Did you ever see this blooper which said, "I am their leader! Which way did they go?" At first I laughed then I recalled my classrooms throughout the years parading them down halls, sidewalks, through museums, etc. and hoping everyone followed me. What kept them in line? Sometimes it's enough "responsible" students that always do the right thing and strategically placed, I could hope they had some positive influence. At Art Prize, it was an actual rope that everyone held that kept us moving in a large, slow amoeba like fashion.

I wonder what the Lord is thinking when He sees us not following Him. I think I'm better off with some pretty concrete "ropes" to hang onto to keep me where He wants me to be. My ropes come through Scripture, other people, and prayer.

Unlike most of our students who think they have a better way or just like the freedom to go their own way, I choose the rope. I'm safe and loved there. Hopefully your students will feel safe and loved with you as well as they follow their leader. And you follow yours! Be blessed by the Lord and highly favored.

Are You Happy or Joyful?

Do you consider yourself a "happy" person? Or does your attitude depend on your circumstances? What kinds of things make you happy? Most of us probably share a common list of "happy." (Vacations, gifts, time to relax, time with family, a new boat…) But what makes you happy when the gift isn't new, the family goes home, time gets taken up with real life, and the boat becomes a responsibility instead of fun? Are you still "happy"?

Each one of these things could be considered part of this world; earthly, fleeting, things we won't take with us when we leave this earth. Not to say there's anything wrong with any of these. But then where does our happiness come from?

I want to explore what we're really looking at. Nowhere in the Bible does God promise us happiness. What it does say in many places is "joy." I'm thinking that happiness and joy are two different things. Lots of things make me happy but the feeling doesn't last. Something ends or changes and so does my mood. But does it have to? Not if, as it says in Nehemiah 8:10, "The joy of the Lord is your strength." When my joy comes from the Lord, the knowledge of my salvation, His greatest gift, then like Paul, I can know "that to live is Christ and to die is gain." In other words, it's all good. My joy is in knowing Christ, my Savior, Friend, Redeemer, my Constant Companion, A Fountain of Unending Love, and yes, the Source of my true joy.

That means that even when my earthly happiness is threatened or squelched, my heart will still be filled with the joy of the Lord. As a follower of Christ, my life should reflect that. What will that look like as I walk through my day today? Will people think I'm happy, or are my circumstances dictating my attitude? What they could see is not happiness but pure joy. Joy in the Lord.

Romans 15:13: "May the God of hope fill you with all joy and peace as you trust in him, so that you may overflow with hope by the power of the Holy Spirit." Be blessed by the Lord and highly favored.

Fear

A dictionary definition: an unpleasant often strong emotion caused by expectation or awareness of danger; anxious concern, worry. Or a reverential awe esp. of God.

Synonyms: dread, alarm, fright...

We read the word "fear" many times in the Bible. But often it's in the context of "Do not be afraid." Angels appear unexpectedly and the first thing they say is, "Do not be afraid." It makes it sound as if in that particular situation, the angel anticipated that the person being addressed would naturally be afraid.

What things cause fear within us? Anxious concerns and worries plague us at work, with our kids, while we or our family are traveling, there's a baby being born, a surgery, an evaluation, someone's observing in our room...all anxious concerns.

But what do you think Jesus would say to you if He walked into your room now? Probably, "Do not be afraid." He wants to take all the dread, alarm, and fright out of our lives. So, what does He replace it with? His peace, His ever abundant and always available love, and as much of His strength as we need for the day; or for the next hour.

In relating the concept of fear with our faith, I think the opposite might be "trust." Psalm 27 vs.1 says, "The Lord is my light and my salvation..." The Light that casts out fear. And it's at our disposal. A reverential fear, yes, but not an anxious concern. That is not God's desire for us. Trust is. Be blessed by the Lord and highly favored.

Finding Favor

What do you think it looks like when you "find favor"? It's probably not an expression you hear every day. But I believe it can mean a variety of things.

About 27 yrs. ago, I walked into a school building with my 2 girls. It was a new school to us and it was January; an awkward time to enroll. I was nervous and my girls were too. We walked into the office and faced strangers. We knew no one. One teacher walked up to us and looked at my younger daughter with a huge smile, and said, "What grade are you in?" My daughter replied, "Third." "Oh," the teacher said, "I hope you're going to be in my third grade!"

That was all I needed to hear. I knew my daughter would be taken care of and it felt like we had somehow "found favor" with at least one person in that school. From then on, in the buildings in which I taught, I would recite that same script, hoping the student and parent would feel what I felt that day long ago.

My daughter did nothing to find favor with her new favorite teacher. She just showed up. I think that's what happens when we show up for God. We make ourselves available and He shows us favor. Believers have an automatic "favor" just because we believe. I can't be perfect. I was born with sin and sin is my nature. But forgiveness and mercy make up the "favor" given to me because of who my Savior is. I can do nothing to gain it; just like my daughter did nothing to gain favor from her new teacher.

Can I please God? Of course, I can. Can I seek to be obedient? Absolutely. Will I be blessed for this kind of behavior? Yes, that's what He wants to do. Just like we, as teachers, love to give rewards, love to encourage, love to be listened to, so does our Father love to encourage and bless us.

So, I would ask you to look for someone in your path today to whom you can pass that favor. You will be the one receiving the blessing. Be blessed by the Lord and highly favored.

His Plan for You

It's no secret that planning is a huge part of being a teacher. Depending on how diligent you are in your job and what your job is, planning could be a big part of it even if you're not a teacher. So, what's the big deal? Why is planning so important?

I suppose if I asked that question of 10 people I would get 10 different answers but maybe many would agree that planning helps the odds that you'll be more focused on the objective of the lesson and you'll stay on track and quite possibly someone will learn something! At the very least, that may be a reason for planning. You carefully think, read, consult, write, adjust, rewrite, read some more and voila! Your plan is ready. Notice I said "carefully." Good planning IS done with care.

If we are careful about our planning and spend a lot of time and effort on just the right ideas and techniques and prepare our hearts out, and we're only human and have definite limitations, imagine the planning that the Lord can do...limitless in power, time, effort, and love. He wants us to be successful. He wants our lives to be full of joy and He wants to be the provider. But we must submit to His plan. We think our students would do better if they would listen, pay attention to us, and follow our directions. That's what the Lord wants from us. We're no different than our kids. He has the plan and He shares that plan when we listen to Him, read Scripture and pray. Let the Lord plan for you. Be blessed by the Lord and highly favored.

Parents at the Door

I remember a time when I was dealing rather harshly with a young boy in my class. He was quite disrespectful, testing me all the time, usually not engaged in learning and I could and did get frustrated with him often.

I don't like the word "harsh" but I was raising my voice and I know the frustration was there so I guess I probably was harsh. As I finished dealing with him, I turned around to see his Grandma in my doorway. (She was raising five of her grandkids and I had had three of them.) She had said nothing to hinder my reprimand and I was rather embarrassed. I spoke honestly to her and said, "Well, there you go, Grandma. You caught me yellin' at your boy." I then shared with her how disrespectful, rude and disruptive her grandson had been all morning.

She walked towards me, gave me a big hug and said, "That's okay, Ms. Quist. You got to do what you got to do. That's alright by me." Then she turned around and walked out the door.

Ever after that I kept that in the back of my mind: "Deal with/talk to/reprimand students as if their mom was standing at the door." But it's hard to remember. Let's go one step further. What if we talked to our students, spouses, friends, parents, children, as if Jesus was standing at the door? What would we sound like then? Would we use the same words, or tone, or act out of frustration?

Here's the truth. Jesus isn't exactly at the door. He's right beside us. He can intercede and feed us the words to use, calm our hearts, give us the peace we need to diffuse or regulate a situation. The battle isn't ours. It's the Lords'. We might as well give it to Him. He's willing to fight it for us and He will always win.

I pray that all through my days, I can stop and look to Jesus next to me, and hand over the battle. I want to learn to look to Him for direction and assurance especially when I'm ready to lose control. I'll act like there's a mom in the doorway but Jesus will be by my side. If I'M in charge, there's no winning the battle. They don't call Him "Savior" for nothing. Be blessed by the Lord and highly favored.

Stillness

When was the last time you were still, besides waiting to fall asleep? I mean really still? Still, as in intentionally mute with a quiet body. Still in anticipation. Waiting. Waiting and listening. Listening for some communication or answer or word, or a prodding…like from the Lord.

Teachers are notorious for many things, but one probably is not being still. And yet, there are times and examples in the Bible where we are told to be still. Psalm 46:10 says, "Be still and know that I am God."

But somehow sitting still has earned a bad connotation; another word for "lazy." Yet how will the Lord get our attention? How will He communicate? How will He teach us or reach us if we don't stop and "be still"? We get our kids' attention, then expound. We ask them to listen, repeat, practice, work in pairs, listen again, and repeat, work quietly, read silently, dig, investigate, reflect, write, rewrite; basically, to be still and learn.

Be still and grow in your knowledge of…whatever.

The Lord is asking us to do the same things. He wants us to be still, to take the time to listen, investigate, read quietly, think, dig, share, and reflect. We would probably agree that it is much easier to teach or at least feel like you're an effective teacher if your students listen quietly but then actively pursue acquiring knowledge. I think the Lord probably thinks the same of us. But we don't always do the quiet listening first.

We're just doers and goers and think we always must be in charge.

God says, "Be still and know that I am God." God is God and I am not. Strength is shown through stillness. Just ask your most hyper students. What's the hardest thing for them to do? When are they strong?

When are we strongest? Blabbing on and on to our students, blabbing on and on at our families? Even reciting our requests to God in prayer...yes, He wants to hear our wants and desires, but do we stop and listen for Him? It's a two-way relationship. When you're still, God can answer. Let your strength be your stillness. Be blessed by the Lord and highly favored.

References

Cowman, L. B. (1997). Streams in the desert. Zondervan: Grand Rapids, Michigan.

MacArthur, J. (2005). The MacArthur bible commentary. Thomas Nelson: Nashville, Tennessee.

Merriam-Webster Dictionary. (2017). Online definitions.

Ogilvie, L.J. (1997). God's best for my life. Harvest House Publishers: Eugene, Oregon.

Quick Verse. (2010). Bible verses. Online resource.

Stanley, C. (2012). In touch. In Touch Ministries: Atlanta, Georgia.

Young, S. (2009). Jesus lives. Thomas Nelson: Nashville, Tennessee.

Acknowledgements

There is nothing in my life I can claim as my own achievement. Either it was directly gifted to me by the Lord, or He used other people to help me. This compilation of God's Word, prayers, devotions and personal reflections, is no exception. I have quoted God's very words, the prayers were generated by the Holy Spirit, the devotions and reflections are from my experiences, and everything that had to transpire to compile, edit, and actually move from computer to paper, was because of Dr. Michele Coyne. Besides being a best friend, colleague and confidant, Michele is an expert on the computer where my knowledge stopped at the composition.

While Michele was the nuts and bolts, my good friend, Nancy Carter, was my constant encourager. She provided the motivation I needed to persevere and not give up. She believed in my mission and never doubted that I could finish it. Without this encouragement from Nancy and the editing, fine tuning and countless hours of putting it "all together" by Michele, there would be no prayer book for teachers. Thank you, my dear and gifted friends.

www.ingramcontent.com/pod-product-compliance
Lightning Source LLC
Chambersburg PA
CBHW071615080526
44588CB00010B/1136